Crystals
and Us

A loving, healing relationship

Dr. Gulrukh Bala, Ph.D

YogiImpressions®

YogiImpressions®

CRYSTALS AND US

First published in India in 2011 by

Yogi Impressions Books Pvt. Ltd.

1711, Centre 1, World Trade Centre,
Cuffe Parade, Mumbai 400 005, India.
Website: www.yogiimpressions.com

First Edition, September 2011

Copyright © 2011 by Dr. Gulrukh Bala

ISBN 978-81-88479-83-2

Printed at: Uchitha Graphic Printers Pvt. Ltd., Mumbai

CONTENTS

FOREWORD

Our relationship with the crystal kingdom

Crystals feel like someone we have known for a long time, like an old and trusted friend with whom each encounter feels like coming home. Working with them can change the way we think and feel. It is like we have had a quiet talk with a wise friend and now things look better. Brighter. Lighter.

Crystals speak the language of light. In this book, Gulrukh Bala shares with us the words of light that the stones speak to us in their silent language of Spirit. She takes us to the heart of the crystal kingdom and shows us a museum of images, punctuating them with the insight and wisdom that only a traveler of deep experience and vision can reveal. She shows us the landmarks of the world of stones, naming each, and makes sure we know the terrain and can find our way back whenever we wish to visit again. Her warm stories share both the excitement of each new crystal encounter and the deep knowing of the messages the stones are sharing.

Discussing the most important and easily available stones and their properties, with Gulrukh we are informed, intelligent visitors to the world of stones. Soon we know them all like the back of our hand. As our guide, Gulrukh shows us how to work with the stones as if they contain all the best kept secrets that the visitor seeks, but that only those who call the streets of the city their home, can truly know about.

There are many books that tell us about stones, their healing properties and their structures. This little jewel of a book does this too, but more than this, Gulrukh weaves her words for us into guidance that is as personal as a hand drawn map. She walks with us every step of the way pointing out exactly how each turn along the path leads us further along our journey with crystals, as we find our own personal and unique destination. Whether we seek healing, enlightenment, a deeper connection to Spirit or a true life story about these things, each page is a stepping stone along a journey of learning, listening and living in the world of stones.

Having a guide book in hand and walking with a guide at our side are two very different things. This book is both. With pages of easy to read definitions and exquisite photographs, Gulrukh takes our hand and strikes the delicate balance of knowledge and wisdom that is necessary for those who wish to tour the paradise of the crystal kingdom, seeking to call it their new hometown.

Working with crystals solely by learning their names or identifying them in a photograph is limiting. The learning begins with these gentle lessons in a synergistic fashion, as the author combines these important pieces of the puzzle which then become the whole that is more than the sum of its parts. As we turn the pages, our connection will begin to form and reveal insights. As our intuition develops we begin to see with new eyes and to listen with intent to a silent language being whispered to us as if it were our mother tongue. This is the silent language of crystals and the messages they wish to share with us, that Gulrukh guides us to understand.

Practical and useful grids, layouts and combinations are thoughtfully planned for us, as if each were a day trip filled with exciting sights, new tastes and experiences as well as a personal audience with the ambassadors of the stone kingdom seated at our own reserved table. We experience a newfound confidence with Gulrukh leading us, and soon we are ordering off the menu all the delights of the city as if we were locals.

I believe that Gulrukh gives us an attunement to the energies of the stones not only through the exquisite photographs, but by gently opening our hearts as she infuses us with her deep peace and wisdom with her words. Her connection to the crystal kingdom is our ticket to a journey filled with fair winds and a gentle current that carries us home to a place we find we have hardly ever left. The Emerald City* of our waking dreams. The crystal kingdom.

'Crystalistener'
Liz Connell
Crystalightworker
USA
www.crystalistener.org

---

* Reference to the book *The Wonderful Wizard of Oz* by Frank L. Baum, in which the main character, Dorothy, is taken on a journey to a magical place of her dreams: The Emerald City.

INTRODUCTION

My relationship with crystals

Crystals have brought immense Light into my life. I remember I was all of eleven when we were taken by Queen Mary School on a weekend geology trip to the beautiful hill station of Panchgani.

The table land, the scenic beauty and particularly the beautiful rocks that lay strewn on the paths captivated me! I started thinking about the stellar beauty lying within those rocks and stones I saw wherever we walked. I had an empty lunch box with me – just the right thing to have – and in this I placed the stones that I had begun picking.

When I got home, I happily scrubbed them and wiped them clean of all the caked red soil that they had probably collected for decades. My mother encouraged me to place the rocks on the pelmets of our high-ceilinged living room. They became the centre of attraction and quite a conversation piece. It was only much later that I learned their names – clear quartz and amethyst, gleaming sentinels that gave me such happiness!

At the age of twelve, I remember wearing my mother's

special strand of green stones around my neck – light green stones whose facets sparkled in the light and dark green ones that had the smoothest texture to them. 'What were these divine stones?' I wondered.

I loved that light green necklace and wanted to take it away from my mother and wear it. However, I restrained myself, for my mother treasured it, kept it safely and wore it on special occasions with her elegant saris. I learned many years later that these light green jewels were peridot crystals cut in hexagons and faceted. The dark ones were green aventurine.

Things fell in place after I attended a Crystalline Ascension workshop in 1997. This experience confirmed to me very soon that I already knew what crystals held inside them and I was sure that in a previous birth I had lived in Lemuria* where I had used this vibrational frequency to add richness to my life.

At the workshop, I bought some crystals and when I came home that evening, I had a healing session with a friend. As she lay down, I discovered how comfortable I was with using crystals to balance her chakra field and to clear the grey energies. It made me wonder how I was so skilled at it. It was as though a dormant wellspring had opened up.

---

* Lemuria was an ancient civilisation that existed prior to and during the time of Atlantis. It is believed that Lemuria existed largely in the Southern Pacific, between North America and Asia/Australia. Lemuria is also sometimes referred to as Mu, or the Motherland (of Mu). At the peak of its civilisation, the Lemurian people were both highly evolved and very spiritual. While concrete, physical evidence of this ancient continent may be hard to find, many people 'know' that they have a strong connection with Lemuria.

The next morning I called a friend and explained my urgency to go crystal shopping right away. She said she knew just the place. Right next to her laundromat, there was a crystals warehouse where most of the rocks were dumped outside the shop. We went there and it was a feast for sore eyes! I got home three cartons filled with natural amethyst and clear quartz rocks. This was the beginning of many fulfilling years!

In the year 2000, I was invited by a store in South Mumbai to place my healing crystals there. I did so. The next day there was a long line of people coming up to me with many questions. I returned home tired, but very happy.

The following day the queue doubled. It so happened that two women asked me: "Dr. Bala, where is your book?" 'What book?' I asked myself. It set me thinking and culminated in this simple little book.

The books were soon out of stock. I decided that I would somehow find the time to create a second, revised edition. I had been busy teaching from home, grooming young lives from 1995, and it is only recently that I came back to the book again. This revised edition is in your hands now and as you read it, you will experience a whole new world of opportunity opening up, one in which you can avail of deep core healing and transformation.

There is a special place for crystalline healing deep at the centre of my being. Each crystal and stone has a precious property and each has a story to tell. Each has a healing energy to offer. As we allow this energy to flow into our being, we fill ourselves up and overflow into our world with life-giving goodness in each breath.

It is unfortunate that we hardly understand or acknowledge the gracious ways of God who has so abundantly filled the bowels of beloved Mother Earth with precious healing energies. Such is her plenitude and munificence, and such is our heaped human transgression! In our ignorance we pollute her layers, contaminate her surface and desecrate her sacred vibratory frequency.

Beyond belief and comprehension, our heartless response to Mother Earth's heartfelt love and constant care leaves a sensitive human gasping.

We are humbled in repentance to our sacred Earth energies which are so replete with perfection in all ways. Ageless and timeless are her treasures – pure metals and minerals abound in her. Lustrous riches of healing wealth dwell in her.

Psychic powers and healing remedies have been the rewards of those seers and sages who, in ancient times, tirelessly strove towards interpreting Mother Earth's secrets of perfection. They knew that all vibratory frequencies manifest in energy and form. Crystals have been known for their natural radiation and electromagnetic properties holding within their core the seed of manifesting our intent – our abundance, health, peace, longevity and more.

Kayakalpa is the time-honoured method for rejuvenating our body at the cellular level using crystalline energies for healing along with herbs and Yogasanas.

India has immense mineral wealth lying unexplored. An infinite variety of healing crystals holding astounding power remains untapped in our country. Her mountains, caves and forests hold within them the power to rejuvenate and transform living. India is the original home of the coveted gem treasures of Persia, Damascus, Samarkand, Bokhara as well as the English crown jewels including the valuable Kohinoor diamond and the precious gems encrusting the Peacock Throne.

Ever so often as I walk across pathways and climb hills and mountains, I have found entire crystal belts at my feet. While climbing the Arunachala mountain in Tiruvannamalai, South India, in 2002, I was fascinated to see deposits of clear quartz crystals everywhere. It was their clear energy that empowered me to climb the mountain all the way to the top, and after the descent I felt refreshed and far from tired, contrary to what I would have imagined. Climbing a stretch of Mount Shasta in California in October 2010, was as empowering and rejuvenating. What natural wealth! The Shivalik Alpine region in the Himalayas has also held me captive – clear quartz belts of ageless, timeless, speechless harmony.

This and similar experiences have inspired me to delve deeper and deeper into crystalline energy work and harness it for the benefit of our world.

Immense gratitude wells up from my heart and I thank you for reading this book, for choosing to heal your life with the energy that we continually receive from our Source.

Enjoy the journey as I do. I wish you well.

God bless you.

– Gulrukh Bala

CHAPTER 1

THE FORMATION
OF CRYSTALS

We are aware of the constant transformation happening in our lives. All over the world, repressive and orthodox belief systems are being rapidly released with the awakening of the inner yearning to enhance our lives, to get rid of our stress and to rejuvenate our *now*. A great many are using the simple and easy power of crystals to reinstate inner harmony and well-being.

Crystalline energy is rooted in the same five elements as ours. Crystals hold more than seventy-five per cent water in them, just as we do. Therefore, we share a strong connection with crystals and wield the same resilience and fortitude as they do. Inner stability is gained easily and most effectively when we place crystals in the auric field of an imbalance.

Crystals have been present from the beginning of time and hold the energy of the universe. They are created when circumstances are right. Within Mother Earth's crust are present rich mineral solutions and gases that have immense heat. Whenever there are fine cracks and fissures formed through weathering, these gases and solutions flow towards the Earth's surface. From a state of superheat to cooling, the agitation settles into stability. A build up of regular, three-dimensional, repeating patterns of atoms begins. These are termed crystal lattices. Within a lattice each atom finds its balanced arrangement.

Crystals grow continually, like plants do. Once their free atoms are all in orderly arrangement, they hold that energy. When the mineral-rich solutions cool further, the pressure drops and a different configuration of elements begins to create other sorts of crystals. Selenite, calcite and turquoise are examples of soft minerals that crystallise at low temperatures whereas the quartz family, diamonds and emeralds are harder minerals that crystallise at a higher temperature and pressure.

Crystals can dissolve and re-crystallise when subjected to any altered conditions – external or mineral. They can remain unchanged for millions of years and they can repeatedly go through transformations, depending on the climatic conditions. How similar are we! We too can remain unchanged and can repeatedly go through transformations, depending on our situations and relationships.

Technology has made great use of crystalline energy. This is because crystals have the ability to quickly adjust and restore their internal stability when faced with external forces of pressure, heat and electricity. Today our space shuttles, cars, clocks and engines all use crystals. Their strong coherence lends an effective order when used.

Crystals expand our consciousness and help improve the quality of our lives, attuning us with the higher Power that created stones as well as us human beings. Crystals, with their beauty, healing and spiritual properties fill the void experienced by mechanical living. Just as we need salt in our food to add flavour and zest to the meal, we require crystalline energy to add to our day's supply of energy. The virtues and special healing qualities residing within stones rub off on us as we begin to restore balance and harmony in our stress-filled lives. Today, science is discovering how this energy holds lasting benefits for those who use it. Crystalline healing is a tested modality that enriches the lives of those who work with its worth. Its simple directness is easy to learn as we go through this book and understand the basic concepts.

Through my long journey with crystalline magic, I am convinced that we have used the wisdom of stones to transform our lives in many previous lifetimes.

A stone attracts us to its energy field with the force of universal Light, and believe me, we are in a relationship before we even become aware of it!

Choosing a crystal depends on our specific need. We can choose a specific stone that can be used for a certain problem area. Expanding our knowledge helps us to discover new stone energies. My greatest joy has been to lovingly collect them on my travels, fresh from the cradle of Mother Earth.

Our intuition, or inner guidance, will always help us. Trusting it, obeying it, the crystal will respond to our energy.

Cities across the world have shops selling all kinds of wonderful crystals. Annual crystal shows and stone fairs attract collectors and merchants. The energy at these events is of a dazzling frequency. Respect the crystalline energy when choosing/deciding to purchase them. Pay for this energy with a happy flow of exchange. Even exchanging a stone for a stone is an excellent way of expanding our collection. It is a journey into Light, bringing tremendous joy.

Sadly, some of our mines have been depleted, affecting the quality of the remaining crystals. For instance, I find that the rich rose pink quartz has now paled in colour. However, it is important to note that the properties of the crystals are always the same.

It is wise to make sure that we are paying the right price for our stones and to avoid purchasing in haste.

Here is a selection which is simple and effective for every home.

- Amber (Pics. 69, 105, 110)
- Amethyst (Pics. 8, 17, 26, 34, 77, 94, 102)
- Black Tourmaline (Pics. 1, 18, 19, 82)
- Clear Quartz (Pics. 2, 11, 16, 19, 31, 62, 64, 73, 78, 91, 102, 103, 104, 109, 111)
- Garnet (Pic. 35)
- Green Quartz (Pic. 68)
- Lapis Lazuli (Pics. 3, 32, 83, 86)
- Malachite (Pics. 4, 87)
- Orange Carnelian (Pics. 66, 75, 93, 102)
- Peridot (Pic. 101)
- Rose Quartz
  (Pics. 15, 27, 33, 67, 76, 81, 85, 89, 90, 102, 104, 106, 107)
- Tiger's Eye (Pics. 30, 84, 108)
- Yellow Agate (Pics. 61, 95)

CHAPTER 2

SPECIAL POWERS LOCKED WITHIN SHAPES OF CRYSTALS

Stones are creations of nature, which have been exposed to weathering by the five natural elements. Crystals take form only when the circumstances are right. Their shapes are quite different when they are first seen. However, they are later cut, faceted, polished and tumbled. This further changes their shape. All naturally shaped stones hold within them immense power. Their shape is therefore very important.

Natural stone formations hold the cosmic force – divine wave patterns. Using such healing stones brings release from all blockages within our being. A stone talks to us powerfully through its natural rock structure.

Holey Stones (Pic. 12)

Stones with natural holes in them are produced through years of erosion by wind and water. They have receptive and protective energies.

They prevent nightmares when placed by the bed or under the pillow.

They bring protection when placed near the front door or in the living room.

They help heal the body because the hole allows the ailment to release from the specific point where the problem lies.

It is good to rub such a stone on the body to ensure healing. Psychic awareness increases when we look through the hole into the moonlight.

Looking through holey stones in broad daylight for a minute at a time improves the eyesight.

Cluster (Pic. 6)

A cluster is a natural rock formation with many points. It works most effectively on our five senses when we hold it in our palms, radiating energy out to the environment while also absorbing our tired, dense energy. It becomes a reflection of ourselves and brings balance to tired nerves. A cluster placed above the crown, as seen in the picture, releases fatigue.

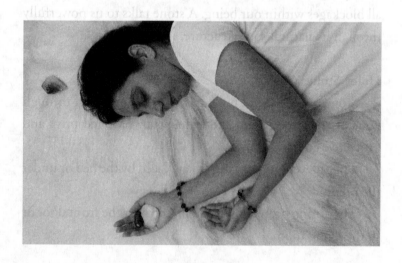

Clusters are especially useful for cleansing a room or other crystals. The crystal that needs cleansing should be left overnight on the cluster.

Round Stones

Round crystals and stones emit energy in all directions. They bring good luck and healing.

The larger they are, the better for psychic communication when used with a pure intent.

Focusing our intent into a round crystal can bring answers to many questions. It is believed that as the moon waxes (growing moon), the crystal ball receives a greater supply of magnetic energy. Our intuition heightens, perception sharpens and thoughts become very clear. We suddenly find ourselves understanding information far more easily than before.

Round stones are linked with the female reproductive system.

Crystal balls have been used by royalty, especially the French, for thousands of years.

Single-pointed Crystals (Pics. 25-31)

A single-pointed crystal is called a generator. It generates or gives out electrical impulses which have a healing effect on us and our world. Its vibrations encircle a large area, triggering growth in all life that is in contact with the Earth, plants and other crystals.

Avoid wearing a single-pointed generator on the body at any given time. This is because the crystal pointing downwards keeps the person engrossed in the mundane energies of the day, without lifting the spirit. Thus, it is very likely that the person feels fatigue more than usual. When the point is set upwards in the pendant, the person tends to live in a dream world and believes all will unfold magically. Therefore, a double-pointed crystal is ideal. This is so because the double points keep the person spiritually uplifted as well as able to enjoy the duties of the day. When we are spiritually grounded in our larger self nature, we perform our duties tirelessly and even have time at hand to pursue our hobbies before we go to bed.

Single-pointed clear quartz generators are very useful for children in their studies. They help enhance focus and concentration when placed on the study table.

They are also useful to eliminate blockages such as low self-worth, lack of confidence, fear and stress, when held in the palms.

This simple technique works easily and quickly to eliminate the above feelings. Actively rotate the crystal pointing outwards twelve times clockwise in the auric field and it will ease stress, body pain and ailments. Pointed inwards, it channels energy to the body. The single-pointed clear quartz generator is to be kept on the student's desk, in front of him as he studies.

Double-pointed Crystals

A double-pointed crystal holds projective energy and integrates spirit and matter. It can be carried or worn on the body to enhance harmony and balance. This crystal creates a continuous cycle of energy by drawing the vibrations up from the physical being and in from the auric sheaths. It breaks old patterns and helps release addictions.

These generators can be placed in our prayer space to clear home energies. They can also be placed on photographs and affirmations for distance healing work.

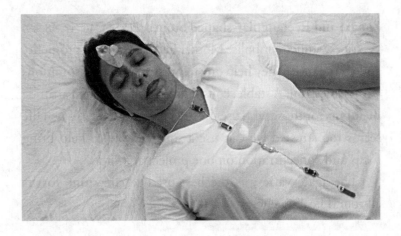

For home protection it is good to hang a clear quartz crystal on the front door or place one before a mirror.

Placed on the Third Eye they enhance telepathy.

Any stone can be used as a double-pointed generator. The most commonly used ones are rose quartz, clear quartz, tiger's eye, green jade, amethyst and black tourmaline.

Oval (Egg-shaped) Stones (Pics. 23, 38, 39, 40, 41, 98)

These stones manifest fresh ideas, stimulate creative energies, detect and correct energy imbalances. When they are used with a pure intent, they promote conception in women. Therefore they are fertility stones.

For a luxuriant garden, large egg-shaped stones should be buried in the soil.

Fertile imagination for artists, students, research workers is generated when oval stones are placed by the bedside.

The most commonly used ones are malachite, smoky quartz and rose quartz.

Square and Rectangular-shaped Stones (Pics. 44, 46, 47, 48, 49)

These stones symbolise Mother Earth energies of prosperity and abundance. They help one to pursue aims and aspirations with dedication. A stable, consolidated and grounded attitude manifests for those who use this shape. For instance, when life seems too stressed we can use a square stone to help bring focus and concentration on one project at a time.

The agate variety is the best used square stone for its all round healing energy.

Heart-shaped Stones (Pics. 88-97, 99)

These stones magnify the love within our spirit and link it to our life. They allow us to receive and give love. They attract a warm loving relationship towards others and us. We begin to understand the wisdom of first loving our own inner beauty before we can hope to help others discover theirs. Love is what makes our world go round. It is the essence of eternity locked into this beautiful shape. A rose quartz heart is the best to enhance love.

Triangular Stones

These are protective stones. They are worn or carried to guard and protect our body energy. In India, many wear a triangular coral for this purpose. Place a triangular stone on the windowsill, preferable facing the street, with the pure intent of protection. A black tourmaline is an excellent choice for this.

Pyramid-shaped Stones (Pics. 85-87)

These stones help a person to concentrate. The pyramid shape helps energies to rise to the apex or tip, towards manifestation and fulfilment of goals and aspirations. It is among the most powerful shapes used for crystalline transmission work.

Here is a useful tip – whenever there is a financial strain, place a currency note of high denomination under a rose quartz or an amethyst pyramid. Now visualise powerfully the money energy flowing upwards from the note to the pyramid, reaching out through the apex into the world and returning to you with abundance.

A pyramid is also favourably used for healing work on the body, drawing off blockages and negative energies and replenishing with vibrant energies. Place a bloodstone pyramid over the photograph of a person who needs healing. Now place an intense intent into the pyramid, programming it for healing. The results are fascinating.

Diamond-shaped Stones

These stones attract wealth and abundance. They are good for everyone to use for alignment of the energy centres.

The *Japa Mala* (Prayer Beads) (Pic. 74)

This strand has one hundred and eight clear quartz crystal beads, which help us to reconnect with our heartlight in a deep way. The round beads help increase our spiritual focus and are therefore very useful for prayer and meditation. The clear quartz has inherent powers of clarity and purity of intent, which help the practitioner.

Green quartz is also used for prayer beads to clear the pain of the past and to heal the present. Yellow agate is used to clear the limiting beliefs that hold one in the material world.

Crystal Necklaces and Headbands (Pics. 65-73)

These beautiful creations have excellent healing properties because of the sheer number worn around the neck. Each specific quality of every stone helps uniquely balance our cellular energy.

For instance, a person wearing an amethyst necklace

will always be protected from the grey energy forces that are all around us. It is important to refer to the qualities of individual stones and their healing effects before wearing them.

Grape Bunches (Pics. 75-80)

These man-made, egg-shaped clusters are custom-made in various stones. They enhance the positive energies in the home, the workplace and on the person (when held in the hands). Some of the important work they do is to relieve stress, release fear, overcome jetlag, bring clarity and confidence, and clear depression. For example, holding a green jade grape bunch in our active palm (the palm we use regularly) for fifteen minutes while we sit quietly concentrating on our breathing, can release several layers of the painful past. Once again, I repeat that it is important to refer to the qualities of individual stones and their healing effects before using them.

Gem Trees (Pics. 100, 101)

These are crystal trees, which are made to enhance the positive flow of energy in our home, study area and office space. A multi-coloured gem tree radiates multiple high energies into the surrounding space. For example, a black tourmaline gem tree will deflect all negativities and maintain exclusive high frequencies of light. It will protect our space. Once again, we will need to refer to the qualities of individual stones and their healing effects before using them.

Rock Slices (Pics. 8-9)

Rock slices are available in several colours and sizes. They are perfect examples of how crystalline energy manifests inside Mother Earth. They make beautiful artefacts which also do the work of clearing the energy of the space where they are placed.

Amethyst Rock Cave (Pic. 13)

This formation holds within it immense power to radiate abundance into our life.

Rainbow Crystal (Pic. 2)

If a crystal has rainbows in it, it is a sign of joy and happiness. It can be used to relieve depression.

Enhydro Crystals (Pic. 2)

Enhydro crystals contain bubbles of liquid that is millions of years old. These crystals symbolise the collective unconsciousness that underlies and unites all things.

Extremely Clear Quartz Cystals (Pic. 103)

These crystals are symbols of alignment with cosmic harmony. Keeping such a crystal aligns our energies to the spiritual realm.

Phantom Crystal (Pic. 31)

Within the body of a larger crystal there appears a ghostlike crystal. A phantom has absorbed learning over eons of time and therefore helps put the past into perspective, overcoming stagnation and pointing the way towards growth.

CHAPTER 3

CRYSTALS AND THEIR PROPERTIES

AGATE (Pics. 9, 50, 51, 52, 53, 54, 55, 56, 57, 58, 59, 60, 61, 63, 102)

An agate stone can be banded, brown or tawny, green, moss, red, black and white, black, grey, and blue lace.

An agate empowers a person with strength, courage, love, healing, longevity, protection, and also improves plant growth.

It increases fertility in women.

It helps overcome spite and envy easily because the stone helps us to love ourselves well enough to release ill-will towards others.

An agate ensures truth in relationships and a healthy circulation in the body.

It guards against skin diseases.

It also prevents insect bites, snake and scorpion stings.

An agate calms and refreshes the body, mind, feelings and emotions when held in the active palm for fifteen minutes.

It relieves thirst when held in the mouth and reduces fevers when placed on the forehead.

An agate ensures a healthy garden!

For children, it is a protective stone, keeping them safe from falling and stumbling.

It guards against the evil eye, black magic and sorcery.

An agate is safe to wear for all.

Blue Lace Agate (Pic. 53)

It heals the nervous and skeletal system.

It dissolves old patterns of repression and is especially useful for men to accept their feelings.

It is worn for peace, happiness and to sustain a calm atmosphere at home. It releases the stress of our workday when we gaze on it. As we hold it in our active palm we feel our stress release. It heals the Throat chakra for free expression.

Green Agate (Pic. 57)

Improves decision-making, resolves disputes and promotes flexible feelings and thoughts.

It aids fertility in women. It enhances healing for the eyes.

Black Agate (Pic. 56)

It is a protective stone that lends courage and helps win success in competitions.

Pink Agate

It promotes love between parents and children.

Black & White Agate (Zebra Agate)
It protects against physical dangers when worn on the body.

Banded Orange Agate (Pic. 52)
It eases the stress in our day, protecting us and restoring the body's energy. It therefore releases fatigue.

Moss Agate (Pic. 63)
It releases spiritual blocks and refreshes the soul. Ensures safe delivery to expecting mothers.

It is the gardener's lucky stone which also rejuvenates energy in the defeated and weary. It brings wealth, abundance, joy and longevity. This stone helps make new friends. It brings deep relief when there is a stiff neck. It speeds up recovery, while clearing depression and imbalances. It promotes deep tissue healing. When drinking water is charged in a moss agate bowl, all of the above happens.

Red Agate
It clears etheric blockages, raising the consciousness. It brings peace and calm to the tired heart. It harmonises the circulatory system and prevents insect bites. It brings security and safety. It dispels fear and returns harm back to its source. Removes body heat.

Brown or Tawny Agate (Pic. 60)
It brings success in all situations. It enhances wealth and protects against the evil eye.

The agate is most beneficial when used over the Throat and Root chakras.

AMBER (fossilised resin, golden brown or yellow)
(Pics. 69, 105, 110)

Amber has been used in beads and pendants since ancient times.

It is the fossilised resin of coniferous trees and often contains specimens of plants and insects that fell into the sticky resin centuries ago.

Being a fossil, it is related to the five elements and therefore associated with time and longevity. It is often transparent or translucent.

It develops peace, trust and wisdom.

It is said to heighten protection and cure ailments.

It prevents almost every ailment of the body and is a grounding stone for higher energies.

It reduces fevers, strengthens the eyes, helps during a woman's labour and releases the effects of the evil eye. It helps heal the liver, spleen, stomach, bladder, kidneys, joints, mucous membranes and the gall bladder.

Amber can be placed into our warm bath water for clearing our toxins.

It magnifies the wearer's beauty, enhances happiness and attracts friendships. Little children are made to wear amber beads to protect them and safeguard their health.

It is an expensive fossil but worth investing in for a genuine piece. Wear it for prolonged periods on the throat or wrist.

AMETHYST (purple, violet to lavender)

(Pics. 8, 12, 13, 17, 26, 34, 77, 94, 100, 102, 107)

This is purple quartz, which has been very popular for the past two thousand years.

Amethyst produces serenity and brings peaceful sleep. Place it under the pillow to ensure good rest.

It is the spiritual stone of inner peace.

Its soothing vibrations de-stress us within minutes.

Wear it to ensure a peaceful disposition during the most trying emotional situations.

It facilitates decision-making, bringing in spiritual insights.

It wards off guilt and brings good judgement.

It helps overcome addiction and over-indulgence in any area.

It heals the nervous system and helps dispel anxiety, fear, doubt and anger.

It always helps protect the wearer from the danger of thieves, harm or sickness.

It sharpens the sixth sense, as it is the stone of wisdom which allows the psychic mind to receive and store useful information. It sharpens the wit and increases mental powers. It is therefore excellent for students and teachers.

It allows people to live in the real world according to their aspirations rather than in a world of fantasy.

It promotes selflessness and spiritual wisdom.

It strengthens the love bond between couples.

An amethyst brings business success and ensures victory in legal matters.

It is our best friend when we are deeply hurt, because it can absorb all our grey feelings.

It transmutes lower energies into the higher frequencies of spirit.

When we face such a situation, we need to cleanse our amethyst overnight in salt water.

When moistened with saliva and rubbed on the face, it ensures a smooth, pimple-free skin.

The chakras that benefit the most are the Throat, Third Eye and the Crown.

An amethyst helps people make a smooth transition and move on when their time has come.

AQUAMARINE (green-blue) (Pics. 44, 46)

The ancient sea goddesses were linked to this stone. It is the stone of purification, peace, psychic expansion and courage. It protects against pollutants.

It is a semi-precious, pale blue-green stone holding the water element. Wearing an aquamarine allows the consciousness to expand, bringing soothing calm, peace and happiness in relationships.

It is useful for closure, as it brings communication from a higher plane.

It brings much joy in a marriage. Therefore it is an appropriate gift to be exchanged by the couple.

It protects during voyages and has been used as a special amulet against storms at sea.

It aligns our physical and spiritual body. It heals our immune system.

It ensures good health, strengthens courage and brings mental alertness. Thus it is an excellent stone for students. It relieves stomach ailments, toothaches, eyes, throat and jaw pain. The Throat chakra is best linked to the aquamarine.

AVENTURINE (green, blue, peach, brown, red) (Pic. 72)

The green aventurine strengthens the brain cells, clearing our vision. It enhances creativity, intelligence and increases healing. The blue aventurine opens up the Throat chakra releasing rigid points of view and bringing honest communication with ourselves.

The aventurine is a very good stone for students. Taped to the cell phone, it protects us from harmful electrical emanations.

It is a fine stone for good luck. The Solar Plexus and Heart chakras are best linked to the aventurine.

BLOODSTONE (Pics. 29, 96, 108)

The bloodstone is deep green, flecked with red or yellow jasper.

It has been used for the last three thousand years.

It banishes evil and negativity.

Its most important use is to stop the bleeding when it is pressed on a wound. Soldiers have frequently carried it as first aid.

Its cool temperature helps cure all blood related ailments and nosebleeds.

Placed in a glass bowl filled with water, by the bed,

we are ensured of peaceful sleep.

Athletes have worn it to increase stamina.

It lends longevity, peace, courage and fearlessness.

It encourages selflessness.

A bloodstone brings victory in legal matters and attracts wealth when placed in the cash drawer.

It eliminates anger and detoxes the liver, kidneys, spleen, bladder and intestines.

It heals stammering, nervous conditions and stimulates perception and creativity. It bring together our thoughts and feelings. It heals the heart and brings rejuvenation.

It heightens intuition and creativity. It stimulates the immune system especially when placed over the thymus.

It heals ancestral lines, realigning their energies to the Source.

It also helps in farming.

It prevents miscarriage and eases childbirth. It is a protective stone, which keeps us hidden from the eye of a prowler. Taped to a cell phone, it protects us against its emanations. The Root chakra is best linked to the bloodstone. Wear daily for wellness.

CARNELIAN (red, pink, orange, brown)
(Pics. 66, 75, 93, 102)

A red carnelian grounds and guards the wearer. It promotes harmony and dispels anger, envy, resentment and depression.

It brings courage and inner strength.

It is an excellent stone for the timid as it releases the

fear of public speaking.

The carnelian brings eloquence, self-confidence and clarity to the wearer as it overcomes negative conditioning.

It removes doubts and negative thought patterns.

When worn on the body it clears all circulatory disorders related to the kidneys, bones, ligaments, body fluids, skin ailments, nosebleeds, and keeps the mind in balance.

It protects the home and brings in abundance. It prevents nightmares when placed under the pillow. It protects against rage, envy, resentment – ours as well as that of others. The Sacral and Navel chakras are best linked to the carnelian.

CAT'S EYE (Pic. 41)

Cat's eye is luminous opalescent quartz.

It holds the Earth energies and is worn to increase beauty and youthfulness.

It helps enhance wealth and restores lost wealth to the wearer of the stone.

It brings excellent luck and financial gain.

It helps clear the vision, keeps the mind sharp, releases depression and heals the body.

✦ CITRINE (golden-yellow, yellowish-brown or smoky grey-brown) (Pics. 7, 65, 102)

This beautiful golden yellow stone holds the fire element and belongs to the topaz family.

It is a stone of abundance.

It absorbs, transmutes and grounds all negative energies.

It is a powerful cleanser and regenerator.

It removes fears and nightmares and protects the wearer.

It invigorates.

It ensures good sleep when placed under the pillow.

It is a protective stone and energises every level of life.

It raises self-worth, self-confidence, motivation, constructive criticism and optimism. This dynamic stone attracts abundance and success, overcoming fear, doubt and depression at the deepest levels.

The Sacral and Solar Plexus chakras are best linked to the citrine.

CORAL (Pics. 39, 71)

It is considered a powerful stone for the living in Hindu mythology, as it is believed to contain the life essence of Mother Goddess energies which dwell in the ocean in the coral reefs.

In the Pacific islands, temples have been built out of coral.

It is the skeletal remains of sea creatures and brings healing, peace, protection and wisdom.

It comes in many colours, the most common being white, orange, peach and red.

Coral means 'daughter of the sea' in Greek.

Coral's magical power is believed to regulate menstrual flow when worn hidden from the eyes of men.

It protects against the evil eye, accidents, violence, theft and sterility in women.

Coral brings many internal changes. For instance, it

strengthens the nervous system and brings wisdom and clarity.

If young children wear coral, it eases the pain of cutting teeth. When placed in fields, it protects crops from the ravages of weather and pests.

It is a good luck charm when used at home or in our workspace. It guards against storms at sea.

CLEAR QUARTZ (Pics. 2, 11, 16, 19, 31, 62, 64, 73, 78, 91, 102, 103, 104, 109, 111)

The clear quartz crystal is best known for its psychic healing power and is a stone worth buying. It is said to possess the highest healing energy.

It holds the fire and water element within it.

In the modern world, it is used in commercial business.

A clear quartz crystal double-pointed pencil, when worn on the body, increases psychic powers. It relieves fatigue.

It reduces toothaches, fevers, diseases, and brings harmony to the body energies.

Drinking from a clear quartz crystal cup increases immunity. Drink the charged water every morning to cure ailments. The liver strengthens and the entire body reaches a high immune level.

Clear quartz guards the wearer and the home.

It is wonderful to create our own crystal garden or sacred space by placing several quartz crystals – agate, amethyst, carnelian, citrine, jasper, rose and onyx with clear quartz in the centre.

The Crown is best linked to the clear quartz crystal.

Green Quartz (Pic. 68)

It has a very receptive energy and brings prosperity to the wearer. It enhances creativity by stimulating the intelligent mind. It heals the pain of the past when worn on the body.

It maintains abundance and heals our vision.

Rose Quartz

(Pics. 15, 27, 33, 67, 76, 81, 85, 89, 90, 102, 104, 106, 107)

Its receptive energy stimulates love for ourselves and others. This gentle, warm stone attracts loving relationships and brings compassion to the wearer.

It promotes peace, happiness and stability in a relationship and in the home.

A rose quartz heart in the bedroom increases fertility in women. Place a rose crystal in every room of the home to increase family harmony. It is the best crystal to open the Heart chakra.

Smokey Quartz (Pics. 6, 25)

Its receptive energy enhances the mood by releasing all negative feelings and depression. It grounds the wearer, clears cancers. It heals all ailments and helps manifest goals.

DESERT ROSE SELENITE
(translucent sandy, white and green) (Pic. 21)

The vibratory frequency of this crystal brings psychic, telepathic powers and clears the etheric field of all stale conditioning. It strengthens our affirmations.

DIAMOND (clear white, yellow, blue, pink, brown) (Pic. 45)

The vibratory frequency of this dazzling firestone brings energy, abundance, courage, strength, healing, protection, reconciliation, peace and spirituality. It brings life into life! It enhances love, commitment and fidelity.

It is treasured for its beauty the world over.

Its hardness increases physical strength and is believed to bring courage and victory. It protects against the harmful effects of cell phones, when worn as earrings.

The diamond, which is faceted hexagonally, is believed to bring good luck and reconcile discord.

It treats allergies, chronic ailments, vision and metabolism. It re-energises the aura.

It relieves nightmares and encourages sleep.

Used in meditation and prayer moments, it increases high conscious awareness.

It aids spiritual evolution as it activates our Crown, linking it to the Divine White Light. Wear it daily next to the skin.

EMERALD (green) (Pic. 48)

The receptive energies of this brilliant green stone represent the love of our planet.

The emerald powerfully lends inspiration, infinite patience, loyalty, harmony, friendship, protection, love, abundance, intelligence, spirituality and healthy vision to the owner. It is among the most expensive stones available. When programmed for business, it promotes sales and increases public awareness. It heals negative emotions, brings wisdom and discernment.

The wearer finds an increase in understanding and eloquence in speech.

Knowledge flows like a river for the wearer.

It is an all-round healing stone.

It heals malignant conditions. Wear it on the heart or the little finger of the right hand.

✳ **FLUORITE (purple, green, yellow, clear blue, brown)** (Pics. 20, 99)

It is a projective stone that works with the conscious mind, integrating it to our spiritual nature.

It releases strong thoughts and emotions of anger, desperation and fear. It strengthens the mind and emotional field, so that the wearer gains a clear, calm and confident perspective of the present moment.

It cleanses and stabilises the aura. It provides pain relief, clears infections, viruses, arthritis, rheumatism, nerve pain, wrinkles, flu, colds, sinusitis, painful joints, cellular energy, bones and teeth.

Increasingly worn by young people today, fluorite is a new-age stone, an excellent learning aid which also brings emotional stability. It dissolves rigid points of view and opens up our subconscious. Wear as earrings.

Blue Fluorite

It is effective for the ear, nose, throat and eyes. It expands our spiritual awakening through single-pointed focus on the brain cells.

Yellow Fluorite

It is a support for all intellectual activities. It grounds and stabilises group energies. It assists the liver, clears toxins and cholesterol.

Green Fluorite

It clears negativities, infections, stomach and intestinal disorders and cleanses our thoughts, chakras and aura.

Clear Fluorite

It assists in enhancing the effect of other healing crystals during a healing session, and helps align all the chakras.

Violet Fluorite

It opens our Heart chakra. It treats all bone and bone marrow disorders.

GARNET (pink, red, green, yellow, orange, brown, black)
(Pic. 35)

The projective fire energies of this brilliant red stone bring healing, strength and protection. It re-energises all the chakras.

The wearer feels a boost in vigour, patient understanding and strength of body.

It provides pain relief from arthritis, rheumatism, painful joints and nerve disorders. It helps clear wrinkles and prevents flu, colds, sinusitis and viral attacks. It strengthens bones and teeth. It heals cellular energy.

It removes inhibitions and opens our heart, assisting in developing self-worth.

It clears trauma and fragmented living, fortifying our survival instinct. It is linked with our pituitary gland, stimulating an expansion of consciousness.

The protective energy strengthens the aura, repelling all the dark energy fields around, especially against thieves.

Wear a garnet while travelling, to ensure safety.

It also regulates blood pressure, balances the heart and relieves inflammation on the skin's surface.

A garnet should be worn by all those who teach and inspire, because it helps the spoken word to be well received by listeners.

Garnets exchanged while parting stand for love, which will once again bring a happy meeting.

It regenerates and stimulates our metabolism and blood circulation. It heals cellular as well as spinal energies.

Wear it on ear lobes, heart or fingers.

GEODES (Pic. 10)

The receptive water energies of a geode bring fertile thoughts to the user.

They are helpful for meditation, childbirth and fertility.

Geodes are hollows containing crystalline energy.

When sliced, geodes reveal elaborate patterns of minerals, revealing a mass growing inwards.

An amethyst or any other geode can be used in meditation as our object of contemplation. Concentrate on the powers of the stone and visualise the release of the same power towards the manifestation of the goal.

When placed in the bedroom and programmed, a geode can increase fertility.

For students, it can increase concentration and focus.

In the office, it will increase business prospects and success. A geode also helps birthing at the right time, by avoiding a miscarriage.

Write affirmations on a tiny piece of paper, fold it and place it inside the geode. Energise it each morning with a pure intent. This works very well to heal troubled relationships and situations.

IRON PYRITE (golden brown) (Pic. 22)

This gold-coloured mineral is also called Fool's Gold. It offers healing energy, vitality, confidence, positive thinking, will power, manifestation, and clears all negativity. It treats the lungs, bones, circulation, respiration, asthma, and creates cellular healing. It clears the root of an ailment smoothly and easily. Place it at the throat.

JADE (white, cream, lavender, green, blue-green, blue, orange, red) (Pics. 28, 70, 92)

The receptive water energies of this sacred Chinese stone bring protection, prosperity, abundance, wisdom, longevity, purity, serenity, love and healing. It has a soothing energy which helps heal the pain of the past. It holds the significance of wisdom gathered in tranquility.

Jade also empowers weather conditions.

Above all, it works best to prevent body ailments by clearing the underlying roots of thought processes which manifest the ailment. It guards against bladder imbalance and kidney dysfunction. It integrates the mind with the body, encouraging us to become who we really are. It is an excellent kidney cleanser. It assists fertility and child birth. It eliminates toxins and is the best stone for the kidneys. It heals stitches. It balances all our body fluids.

White jade removes all distractions and is excellent for attention-building in children. The Chinese believe that owning jade is more precious than owning gold.

While gardening, bury jade along the boundary of the garden. It brings abundance and nurtures healthy plants.

Jade, when placed on the Third Eye chakra, opens us up to knowledge, strengthening our mind and releasing unawareness. Therefore it is excellent for students.

It guards against mishaps and accidents.

To bring success in business deals, we hold a jade and visualise money entering our life.

JASPER (brown, green, yellow, red, blue and purple)
(Pics. 88, 102)

It protects both physically and mentally. It is termed as the best nurturing stone, unifying and bringing a profound wholeness to life.

It assists in quick thinking, decision making, determination. It facilitates dream recall.

It clears environmental pollution, radiation pollution as well as electro-magnetic pollution.

It helps and strengthens the mind by restraining dangerous desires.

During childbirth, it relieves pain and protects the mother and child when it is worn on the body. It attracts good luck to the wearer.

Green Jasper

It has receptive energies, which help to release obsession and heal the pain of the past. It brings restful sleep and compassion towards others. It stimulates our Heart chakra, clears skin ailments. It reduces inflammation, bloating and releases toxins.

✱ Brown Jasper (Pic. 88)

It is a receptive Earth energy worn for centering and grounding. People who tend to live with their head in the sky should wear a brown jasper. This is also applicable to those in heavy spiritual work.

It strengthens the resolve to give up smoking. It facilitates deep meditation.

Red Jasper

It has a projective fire energy which guards against fever and poison. It deflects negativity completely, and is worn by young ladies to enhance their grace and beauty. It helps dissolve challenges before they become too large. It assists rebirthing, detoxifying and dissolving liver blockages.

Mottled Jasper

It has a projective air energy, which protects against drowning. It is always wise to use it when we are with water energies.

KYANITE (bluish-green, gray, pink, yellow, green and black)
(Pic. 24)

This stone helps in opening and clearing the energies of the body.

It stimulates energy flow, opening up healing circuits. It facilitates dream recall and helps to take necessary measures to release the past. It is a natural pain reliever. It clears fevers, muscular imbalance, the thyroid, the parathyroid, throat, brain, adrenals and the urogenital system. When worn on the body, the divine rays enter to enhance healing.

Epilepsy, paralysis, strokes and any other form of brain-mind imbalances are cleared daily. It supports the body's motor responses and balances the male-female energies in our being. Wear it as a pendant.

$\not\hspace{-0.3em}\uparrow$ **LAPIS LAZULI (royal blue with flecks of golden pyrite)**
(Pics. 3, 32, 83, 86)

This stone has a receptive water energy which brings protection, courage, spirituality, love, constancy, happiness and healing.

It strengthens the bond of love and expands psychic awareness by breaking the barrier between the conscious and the subconscious mind. Thus intuition grows and awareness expands, as it opens the Third Eye.

Children benefit the most because it ensures health, protection, growth, fearlessness and courage.

It is an expensive stone that each one should own and

use. It contacts our spirit guardians. It reverses curses and disease caused by a timid nature of silently witholding pain. It is a powerful thought amplifier. It dissolves suffering, anguish, torture and emotional bondage. It encourages creativity and truth. It releases repressed anger in communication. It clears low blood pressure, vertigo and insomnia. It brings peace, gentle kindness and releases feelings of loneliness.

Lapis lazuli can clear fevers, migraines and blood diseases when worn with a powerful intent.

The Throat and Third Eye chakras are best linked with the lapis lazuli energies. Wear it at the throat.

MALACHITE (green-blue with dark green bands)
(Pics. 4, 87)

This receptive Earth energy empowers a person with peace, inner strength, protection, business success and courage.

It lowers blood pressure, heals swollen joints, vertigo, tumors, fractures, epilepsy, asthma, arthritis, vision, spleen, pancreas, the parathyroid and the immune system.

It combats dyslexia, mental imbalances and psychiatric ailments because it goes to the core of a problem and brings insight.

It is especially helpful in healing trauma from past life sexual experiences. It may cause heart palpitations. Use with awareness.

It is a stone of transformation and draws love to the wearer, guarding against grey energies. Its tranquil green-blue colour is soothing and ensures sleep. It guards us against nuclear radiation rays, electro-magnetic rays and all environmental pollution.

Malachite placed in the cash drawer increases abundance and ensures good business. It is said to prevent falls in children and adults.

Cleanse malachite before and after use by placing it on an amethyst or any other quartz cluster, in the sun. Salt will damage the surface. Wear it on the left hand.

☿ MOONSTONE
(white, pink, green, cream, yellow or blue) (Pic. 38)

This receptive water energy brings protection, youthfulness, love, spirituality, good sleep and an awareness of diet. It is connected with the moon energies. It develops clairvoyance.

Moonstone brings love into our life and clears all misunderstandings between lovers.

Placed under the pillow, it brings restful sleep.

It helps balance excessively aggressive female energies, as also overly aggressive male energies. It balances the menstrual cycle as well as our biorhythm. It calms shock.

We can programme a moonstone with intense intent to work on our food plan, and we will find a definite change.

If I visualise a slimmer, new me who is in full control of a wholesome food plan – as I hold my moonstone in my dominant (active) palm and keep visualising, it will receive my intent and help me work towards it.

It helps digestion, reproduction, breast feeding, clears toxins, heals the eyes, liver, pancreas, hair, insomnia and sleep walking.

Buried in the garden, it brings abundance.

It is a protective stone for swimmers.

Wear it for protection while travelling.

Holding a moonstone in our active palm three days after the full moon and powerfully visualising the future can shape future events. For instance, you can visualise buying a new home. Wear it on the finger or close to your heart.

ONYX (green, red, grey, white, brown, blue, black and yellow) (Pics. 102, 105)

Its projective fire element lends strength and protects the wearer.

It has a marble-like appearance. It heals the blood, teeth, bones, bone marrow and feet.

It protects the wearer during arguments, battles and even on a dark, lonely street at night. It reduces sexual impulses when the partner may be unwell or in the last stages of pregnancy.

It helps when there is a long physical separation between the partners. Onyx acts as a defence against negativity directed towards us, especially supporting through extremely difficult physical and mental challenges. It promotes stamina and steadfastness. It holds memory and can therefore help release past injuries. It clears fears and stress, bringing the precious gift of wisdom.

The Root and Hara chakras are best linked with the energy of this stone.

Wear it on the left finger, around the wrist or the throat.

OPAL (white, blue, green, yellow, orange, red, purple, pink, beige, brown, black) (Pics. 42, 98)

The projective and receptive energy of an opal attracts power, beauty, money, spirituality and fortune.

It contains all the colours and qualities of every other crystal. Therefore, it can be programmed easily.

An opal brings out the inner beauty of the wearer.

We can dedicate affirmations for expanding our inner Light and we will find fortune smiling on us.

An opal develops our psychic powers, brings lightness and spontaneity, strengthens our will power and memory. It clears infections, fevers, diabetes, eye problems, kidneys and the blood.

It changes its shades according to the moods of the wearer. Wear it on your little finger or near the heart.

Fire Opal (orange and red)

It often brings wealth and improves business by attracting customers.

It brings release from deep grief carried over from past lives, as well as helping let go of past pain. It balances and heals the lower body and prevents burn-out.

Black Opal (brown, grey)

This stone empowers the wearer by processing and integrating newly released emotions.

The Root and Hara chakras are best linked with the energy of this stone, as it releases sexual tension arising from painful emotions.

PEARL (Pic. 36)

This receptive Moon energy is the product of a living creature of the waters. An oyster has to be killed in order to remove the pearl lying within. A pearl symbolises Moon and Water energies when it is naturally formed. Today, genuine pearls are very difficult to obtain. Pearls protect the wearer at sea and guard the house against fire. When worn around a ruby, they attract good fortune.

Pearls bring longevity, health, inner strength, courage, fertility, fearlessness and power.

Their different shades denote different attributes.

The **black pearl** with blue tints brings good luck.

The **yellow pearl** brings abundance.

The **pink pearl** brings comfort and ease.

The **red pearl** enhances the intelligent mind.

Natural pearls are rare to find. Therefore, cultured pearls are used all over the world.

PERIDOT (yellowish-green, olive green, honey, brown and red) (Pic. 101)

This receptive Earth energy brings health, abundance, protection and restful sleep.

It protects against the evil eye, enchantments, terror and delusions.

It heals insect bites and liver ailments. It heals and regenerates tissues. It heals relationships.

The peridot calms raging anger, relieves depression, guilt, obsessions and clears nervous tension. It heals the heart, lungs, thymus, spleen, gall bladder, eyes and intestines. It balances bipolar disorders.

Its green colour attracts abundance.

Set in gold, it is a protective stone which is best worn on the Throat chakra or on areas of specific concern.

RUBY (red) (Pics. 14, 43)

This projective Fire energy protects, invigorates, empowers, and attracts abundance and happiness.

This precious stone has a deep red colour.

It is especially effective in helping accumulate other precious stones.

Once you own a ruby, many other jewels will come your way.

A ruby safeguards the wearer against psychic attacks, ailments, famines, enemies and all grey energies. It also protects the home space. It clears controversies and calms hyperactivity.

It increases the body's warmth and brings new energy to a tired person. It detoxifies the body, heals the heart and improves blood circulation. It stimulates the spleen, adrenals, kidneys and reproductive organs.

It is best worn on the Heart chakra to release all stale patterns of the past.

Wear it on your finger or near the heart.

SALT

This receptive Earth energy protects, purifies, grounds and brings abundance. Salt is a sacred substance deeply connected with creation and life.

Its crystalline energy sterilises, cleanses and purifies our space. It is used to cleanse gemstones by placing them in a bowl of saltwater.

Adding salt to bath water clears doubts, illnesses and worries. Empowered salt takes away all the negative forces when placed in the corners of each room at night.

A bowl of salt placed outside our home, as well as in our workplace, every day after sunset, helps absorb the heavy grey forces around.

Salt intake closes down the psychic centres. Therefore, minimum salt must be used in cooking.

For those who wish to awaken their psychic centres, less salt is advised in the diet. (Pay attention, Indian pickle consumers!)

Salt crystals attract abundance and grounding.

Renew these bowls every night.

Whenever we feel low or unwell, we can place a bowl of crystalline saltwater at our feet and clear our aura thirty times (the action of plucking feathers from a bird and opening up our fist into the bowl without touching it). We should then drain away the water and wash our hands and face.

All the chakras are suited to receive crystalline salt energies.

SAPPHIRE (blue, green, yellow, purple, black) (Pic. 47)

This receptive water energy attracts peace, abundance, love, healing, meditation, empowerment and psychic clarity.

It stimulates the Third Eye which opens up the subconscious mind and expands wisdom.

It promotes peace and releases anger, depression and negativities.

It promotes loyalty and positive interaction, clearing envy and enmity.

It heals the eyes and the body, cools fevers, regulates the glands, strengthens veins, releases frustration and stops nosebleeds.

Thus, the immune system is strengthened.

It is said to return negativity back to its centre.

It guards the wearer from captivity.

It helps in legal matters and removes fraud. (It works only when the wearer is on the right path.)

The most common shades are blue and yellow.

The Throat chakra is best linked to a sapphire.

These properties are held by both the yellow and the blue sapphire. However, it is the yellow sapphire that clears toxins and lends its healing energies to all living beings, whereas the blue, by virtue of its colour, is to be used only for specific energy healing.

Wear it on the finger or at the place best suited.

TIGER'S EYE (brownish-yellow, blue, pink, red)
(Pics. 30, 84, 108)

This projective fire stone is warm, possessing a golden flash of light. It is most useful for clearing personality disorders and mental imbalance. It clears addictions.

It strengthens our conviction, lends protection, increases energy, attracts wealth, fortune, courage and confidence to the wearer.

It helps build a strong immune system, heals our eyes, throat, bones and reproductive organs.

Place it under the pillow for protection and wear it in gold as a ring or a pendant.

The Root and Sacral chakras are best linked to its energies.

✷ **TOPAZ (golden-yellow, brown, green, clear, blue, reddish-pink)** (Pics. 5, 37, 49)

This projective fire energy brings love, abundance, empathy, good fortune, healing, protection and weight loss to the wearer.

It releases envy, disease, injury, fear, greed, anger, madness, dark forces, depression, sudden death, arthritis, rheumatism, accidents, fire, and sleeplessness.

It promotes self-control, honesty and openness.

It regulates digestion and attracts love into our life.

This is a promising stone for people of all zodiac signs.

It brings restful sleep and clears sleepwalking.

It is a stone that brings joy. It helps us remain open-hearted and generous.

It helps with weight loss because it regulates the digestive system.

The Sacral and Solar Plexus chakras are best linked to the energies of this stone.

Wear it on the ring finger.

TOURMALINE (blue, blue-green, brown, green, yellow, pink, red, watermelon and black) (Pics. 1, 18, 19, 82)

Tourmaline is a unique, transparent crystal when viewed from its side and is opaque when seen from either end. It has a variety of shades which project their energies into the wearer.

☀ Red Tourmaline (rubellite)

This crystal energises and protects the body, strengthening will-power and courage. It heals our Sacral chakra and increases creativity. It heals the spleen, liver, heart, muscles and blood.

☀ Pink Tourmaline

This beautiful crystal attracts love, friendship and compassion for others. It inspires us to love ourselves first before we love others. It brings peace, relaxation, compassion and healing.

☀ Blue Tourmaline

It removes stress, dissolving blocks, bringing peace and restful sleep. It is a healer's stone as it prevents negativity from sticking. It helps clear vision and speech imbalance. It promotes fidelity, truth, harmony and selflessness.

☀ Green Tourmaline

This crystal attracts wealth and business success. It enhances creativity in the wearer. It opens the heart and brings balance. It heals the brain, nerves, eyes and thymus. It relieves constipation, diarrhoea, panic attacks and claustrophobia.

Black Tourmaline (Pics. 1, 18, 19, 82)

This is the most protective stone because it deflects all negativity, however strong the force may be. It is excellent for removing the evil eye and extreme ill-will. Wear it at home and at the workplace for best results.

It protects against radiation, electromagnetic smog, cell phones, psychic attacks and spells.

It realigns the spine and protects against all disharmony.

Watermelon Tourmaline

This crystal looks like a slice of watermelon with an inner red or pink hue, encased in green. It balances the male and female energies of the wearer, attracts love, tenderness and friendship. It clears depression and brings peace, patience, diplomacy and joy.

The Root, Sacral and Solar Plexus chakras are best linked to the energies of this stone.

TURQUOISE (green, blue, turquoise) (Pic. 40)

This receptive Earth energy attracts courage, love, friendship, healing, fortune, protection, abundance and security. It is a stone of purification and guards against the evil eye, disease, violence, accidents, dangers and poison.

It attracts new friends, empathy, balance and joy, and enhances beauty. It aligns all the chakras. It heals the vision, removes fevers, headaches, rheumatism and arthritis. It clears exhaustion, depression and panic attacks.

Drinking turquoise-charged water improves the health.

The Throat chakra is best linked to the energies of opening up communication and improving relationships.

Wear it around the throat or where appropriate.

Natural Rock Crystals

Pic. 1
Black Tourmaline

Pic. 2
Clear Quartz Enhydro Rainbow
Channeling Crystal

Pic. 3
Lapis Lazuli

Pic. 4
Malachite

Pic. 5
Yellow Topaz

Pic. 6
Smokey Quartz Cluster

Pic. 7
Citrine

Pic. 8
Amethyst Rock Slice

Pic. 9
Agate Rock Slice

Pic. 10
Clear Quartz Geode

Pic. 11
Clear Quartz
Natural Angel

Pic. 12
Holey Amethyst

Natural Rock Crystals

Pic. 13
Amethyst Rock Cave

Pic. 14
Uncut Ruby

Pic. 15
Rose Quartz

Pic. 16
Clear Quartz

Pic. 17
Amethyst

Pic. 18
Black Tourmaline
with Mica

Pic. 19
Black Tourmaline with
Mica and Clear Quartz

Pic. 20
Fluorite

Pic. 21
Desert Rose Selenite

Pic. 22
Iron Pyrite

Pic. 23
River Valley Stone

Pic. 24
Kyanite

Generators

Pic. 25
Smokey
Quartz

Pic. 26
Amethyst

Pic. 27
Rose Quartz

Pic. 28
Jade

Pic. 29
Bloodstone

Pic. 30
Tiger's
Eye

Pic. 31
Clear
Quartz

Gemstones

Pic. 32
Lapis Lazuli

Pic. 33
Rose Quartz

Pic. 34
Amethyst

Pic. 35
Garnet

Pic. 36
Pearl

Pic. 37
Blue Topaz

Pic. 38
Moonstone

Pic. 39
Red Coral

Pic. 40
Turquoise

Pic. 41
Cat's Eye

Pic. 42
Opal

Pic. 43
Ruby

Pic. 44
Pale Blue Aquamarine

Pic. 45
Diamond

Pic. 46
Light Blue Aquamarine

Pic. 47
Yellow Sapphire

Pic. 48
Emerald

Pic. 49
Brown Topaz

Agate

Pic. 50
White Agate

Pic. 51
Gray Agate

Pic. 52
Banded Orange Agate

Pic. 53
Blue Lace Agate

Pic. 54
Blue Gray Agate

Pic. 55
Orange Agate

Pic. 56
Black Agate

Pic. 57
Green Agate

Pic. 58
Blue Green
Flecked Agate

Pic. 59
Camel Agate

Pic. 60
Brown Agate

Pic. 61
Yellow Agate

Bowls

Pic. 62
Clear Quartz Bowl
for energising
drinking water

Pic. 63
Moss Agate Bowl
for energising
drinking water

Massager

Pic. 64
Clear Quartz Massager
for vita-flex points

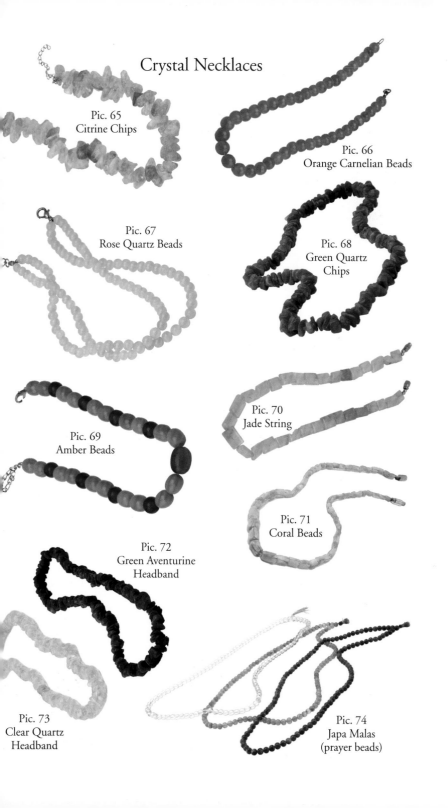

Crystal Necklaces

Pic. 65
Citrine Chips

Pic. 66
Orange Carnelian Beads

Pic. 67
Rose Quartz Beads

Pic. 68
Green Quartz
Chips

Pic. 69
Amber Beads

Pic. 70
Jade String

Pic. 71
Coral Beads

Pic. 72
Green Aventurine
Headband

Pic. 73
Clear Quartz
Headband

Pic. 74
Japa Malas
(prayer beads)

Grape Bunches

Pic. 75
Orange
Carnelian

Pic. 76
Rose Quartz

Pic. 78
Clear
Quartz

Pic. 77
Amethyst

Pic. 79
Jade

Pic. 80
Smokey Quartz

Double-pointed Pencil Pendants

Pic. 81
Rose Quartz

Pic. 82
Black Tourmaline

Pic. 83
Lapis Lazuli

Pic. 84
Tiger's Eye

Pyramid-shaped Stones

Pic. 85
Rose Quartz

Pic. 86
Lapis Lazuli

Pic. 87
Malachite

Hearts and Healing Pendants

Pic. 89
Dark Rose
Quartz

Pic. 88
Brown Jasper

Pic. 90
Light Rose
Quartz

Pic. 92
Jade

Pic. 91
Clear Quartz

Pic. 93
Orange Carnelian

Pic. 94
Amethyst

Pic. 96
Bloodstone

Pic. 99
Fluorite Heart

Pic. 97
Lapis Lazuli

Pic. 95
Yellow Agate

Pic. 98
Opal

Gem Trees

Pic. 100
Amethyst
Gem Tree

Pic. 101
Peridot Gem Tree

Crystal Grids

Pic. 102
Abundance Grid made of
Agate, Amethyst, Carnelian,
Citrine, Jasper, Rose, Onyx,
Clear Quartz in a glass bowl

Pic. 103
Clear Quartz Cube
with 54 Pyramids
for fearlessness

Pic. 104
Peace and Harmony Grid
made with an assortment of
Rose Quartz and Clear Quartz
crystals in a glass bowl

Bracelets and Anklets

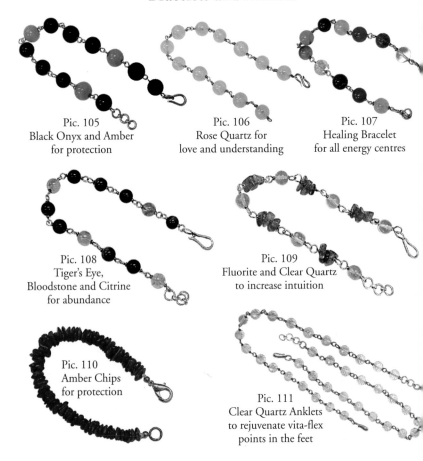

Pic. 105
Black Onyx and Amber
for protection

Pic. 106
Rose Quartz for
love and understanding

Pic. 107
Healing Bracelet
for all energy centres

Pic. 108
Tiger's Eye,
Bloodstone and Citrine
for abundance

Pic. 109
Fluorite and Clear Quartz
to increase intuition

Pic. 110
Amber Chips
for protection

Pic. 111
Clear Quartz Anklets
to rejuvenate vita-flex
points in the feet

CHAPTER 4

CRYSTALS AND
THEIR COLOURS

Colours have immense healing power. Our world is colour. As we begin to awaken to the world of colour, we actually become conscious of the energising effect colour has on us. Each thought and feeling, each breath and emotion is coloured with the colour we choose.

It is for this reason that we are drawn to pearlescent silver white when we introspect and discover the joys of time spent alone with our spirit.

Dull and drab colours often attract an imbalance into the aura.

Let us look at colours from the perspective of chakra healing.

GREEN
(Pics. 4, 20, 28, 48, 57, 63, 68, 70, 72, 74, 79, 87, 92, 101)

It is the colour of grounding and balancing, which keeps us attuned to Mother Earth energies. It is the colour of fertility and of life itself. It prevents migraines, strengthens vision, heals the kidneys and stomach, and promotes conception.

It attracts abundance and good fortune. The person grows in peace, sincerity and frankness because of the qualities of trust, hope, balance, joy and harmony. However, rigid points of view are likely to be developed too.

RED (Pics. 35, 39, 43)

This active, projective colour holds the energy of inner strength. It strengthens will and determination, lends courage and energises the wearer. It keeps thoughts pure and clear, guarding against violence and anger.

It is the sacred colour of blood and therefore, birth.

Red stones therefore can prevent miscarriage, relieve anaemia, heal wounds and stop bleeding. It is the colour of a happy person; however, a confused or selfish individual could well use the dynamism of red towards futile and self-centred goals.

PINK (Pics. 15, 27, 33, 67, 76, 81, 85, 89, 90, 106)

This is the colour best suited to love ourselves – to accept responsibility for our role in life and to release what needs to go, so that we move forward in our days.

It is only then that others can receive our love offering.

The pink energy is packed with soothing, calm vibrations of love which de-stress and refresh us, keeping us protected from a painful past swallowing our future.

Difficulties in relationships are tided over and openness is forged for the future.

ORANGE (Pics. 66, 69, 75, 93, 102, 107)

This projective energy illumines the heart and mind, empowering the spirit to tap into Divine Light.

Orange expands self-worth and conscious awareness.

It attracts fortune and success.

However, insincere tendencies may arise in the user.

YELLOW (Pics. 7, 61, 65, 74, 95, 107, 108)

This projective colour brings eloquence in expression.

Its protective air energy strengthens the conscious mind and heightens the ability to visualise powerfully.

The nervous system, digestion and skin are nourished and strengthened by this colour.

It expands mental awareness and energy.

Wisdom, zeal, willingness and flexibility open up for the user.

However, there is a tendency for selfishness and anger to surface.

BLUE (Pics. 3, 32, 37, 40, 44, 46, 53, 54, 58, 83, 86, 97, 99)

This receptive water energy promotes peace, emotional calm, restful sleep, healing, purification and responsibility.

The person becomes more allowing, faithful, self-controlled, spiritual and serious.

There is, however, a chance of holding rigid viewpoints and an introverted nature.

INDIGO (Pic. 3)

This colour enhances focus, discrimination, intuitive awareness, creativity, intellectual expansion and excellent self-expression. It can, however, pull the person down with the ego-self. The ego-self is part of the package which comes with our human birth. It holds within it, our thoughts, emotions and feelings. Constant inner work is needed to free ourselves from its entanglement.

VIOLET (Pics. 8, 12, 13, 17, 26, 34, 77, 94, 102)

This is the colour of peace and healing which maintains health and promotes obedience. Headaches, hair-loss and brain ailments are cleared by utilising violet stones. Meditation, purification and inner peace are enhanced. Generosity, understanding, consideration, sensitivity and broad-mindedness – these are the qualities which the violet stones offer.

WHITE (Pics. 36, 38, 50)

This receptive, protective colour contains all the shades of the spectrum. Therefore, it can be programmed as a worthy substitute for stones of other colours.

BLACK (Pics. 1, 18, 19, 82)

This receptive Earth energy symbolises quiet power, flexibility, and grounding. Colour energy reaches out and connects with our energy through all aspects of our being. We can keep our eyes closed and receive the Light of colour.

CHAPTER 5

CHOOSING OUR CRYSTALS .

It is a joy to choose a crystal that calls out to us. All crystals hold the same internal orderliness and potential for healing even though some of them have inclusions. Inclusions are the grubbiness on the inside of certain stones. Just as we have our strengths and our weaknesses, so does a crystal. Inclusions are there for us as reminders of our own working towards perfection and possibilities.

Some crystals are soft and even brittle while others are hard. Start with a basic collection of stones which are available for a reasonable price. We can increase our range of stones by exchanging them with those who wish to share theirs with us. It is a wonderful way of energy exchange as we find ourselves selecting crystals according to our emotional and physical balance as well as our mental and spiritual awareness levels.

It is fun too, to collect stones as we travel through our country and our world. It is magical how crystals show up at every turn as we climb up a hill or course through a valley floor.

I have collected pristine stones from glacial heights and river beds. Each stone speaks to me its story and calls on me to hold its energy while it unfolds its history. This is the most profound experience of all.

The Colorado has shared with me its immense inner wealth as has the Ganga. The Himalayas and the Grand Canyon have spoken to me, in their language, words of ancient, primordial Light. Mount Arunachala (Meru), has been among my firsts. As I climbed its rocky terrain, I felt an inexplicable energy of Light. It was Lightness. As my questioning grew, I spied clear quartz peeping out at me! More and more of it sprang into view. I was transported into a world of awe. How great is this majestic world of Light! The exhilarating climb in Sedona, Arizona, held the same energies of optimum Light. Yet again, the stones spoke and offered their loving energies – Vaishnodevi in Northern India and the Blue Ridge Mountains in North America have shared with me eternal Time, as have the Appalachian mountains.

At each step I have learned that our beautiful planet is so connected, and every continent, every mountain, every river, every valley is just *One*. An understanding has rooted inside me that I am one with the surge of Oneness. I carry this as deep love within, having been embraced forever in the healing love of stones.

While buying a crystal, we pick one that calls out to us and hold it loosely in our palm. It will begin to resonate with our being, making us feel really alive and happy. A mutual attraction begins.

Curling the tip of our tongue on the roof of our mouth, we create an energy circuit. It is here that our sensitivity is the highest. We may feel the crystal activating certain parts of our body. Warm, tingling sensations may fill our palms. Watch the process. This is our crystalline connection.

Always choose crystals with care, preferably after having attended a workshop and understanding more about them.

If we are familiar with the knowledge of using a pendulum, we can certainly apply it to check if we are buying the right crystal for our energy work.

CHAPTER 6

CLEANSING OUR CRYSTALS

Stones have always been handled by different energies of different people before we bring them into our space. Remember, they have been mined, transported, often polished and then placed in shops and malls for their prospective buyers. These energies need to be removed before working with our stones. Therefore, we cleanse and purify new stones before we use them, restoring them to their original clarity. We release all past influences and patterns from their memory, readying them for our personal use. It should be done each time we use our crystals for healing. If we neglect cleansing, our stones become less effective and may pass on an imbalance. A heaviness hangs in such a space and uneasy feelings rise in those who live there.

There are several simple methods of purification.

The simplest one is holding the crystals under running water and placing them in sunlight for an hour, to enable the beams of light to burn away the past energies. Remember to pick up the stones at sunset if you decide to place them in sunlight for an entire day.

Holding them one at a time in our active palm (the right palm if you are right-handed), we feel the vibrations. We soon receive a strong, healthy, pulsating energy, and know that the cleansing has been done.

For moonstones, pearls, mother-of-pearl and rose quartz, it is good to place them for three consecutive nights in the cool moonlight, as they hold female energies. Check in the same way as described above, to see whether the energies have been replenished. Crystals can also be buried in the soil for several days, to rejuvenate. We can then wash them individually through running water. Another unique way of cleansing is to place our stones on a large amethyst crystal cluster.

An amethyst absorbs negative energies. We can pick up the stone after a day and check its vibratory level in our active palm. Run it through tap water and it is ready for programming. We now need to place our amethyst cluster in the soil or in sunlight for cleansing.

The vibrations of a pure sound will also cleanse the energy of stones. A Tibetan bell or gong can be used.

Deep breaths and then blowing lovingly over the crystal with the intent of clearing its grey energies also works.

Here is the most frequently used method for cleansing a stone: Soak the stones overnight in a glass bowl containing rock salt or sea salt with water. Pick them up in the morning and run them individually through flowing water. It is a convenient and practical method. Avoid this method for soft stones and threaded stones as salt can damage them.

Our crystals are now ready for programming with intent.

CHAPTER 7

PROGRAMMING
OUR CRYSTALS

All of us have been born with infinite potential for positive growth – abilities that are yet untapped and are waiting to be unleashed – the foremost being the potential to programme our thoughts positively. It is this singlemost ability that helps us realise deep fulfilment while we are alive in our body. We are able to prepare our spirit to rise so that karmic issues are washed away when the beams of Light pierce our energy centres and expand our consciousness.

Affirmations are extremely beneficial while programming a crystal. Here is an example – If we wish for excellent results in an interview, we should use the following affirmation when we programme our crystal: "I am clear and confident about my interview."

Here is how to programme a crystal:

Pick out the specific crystal from the cleansing bowl, and run it through flowing water. Now, hold it in the active palm over the heart centre, standing preferably in the sunlight. The beams of ultraviolet light have a cleansing action that enters the crystal and the frequencies of these light vibrations clear the crystal in the best way.

If the crystal has a point, hold it with the point facing upwards. Talk to it, affirming that it is clear of all the previous programming. (It is the same as erasing an old tape.) Our spoken word has done the clearing. At this time, we can blow on the facets of our crystal twelve times clockwise and lovingly give it a name. Whatever the shape, hold the crystal with love and follow the procedure.

Every crystal amplifies energy. Therefore, it is our protective shield.

Here is what we can say for programming our clear quartz crystal: "I am willing to care for you, keep you happy and clean among your family of other crystals. I would like you to give me clarity and confidence. Please maintain all memory of quiet times, meditation, prayer and happy moments so that when I feel low, I can request you to release these peaceful memories, to calm me instantly. When I study, please record the memory of all the work done so that when I appear for my exams, you release for me the memory of all that I have studied. Even if someone else touches you, please maintain my energy field intact within you. Offer me your protective shield, so that only good comes to me. Thank you. God bless you."

Once we have programmed our crystal in this way, all the grey energies and negative thoughts of other individuals in our space, which enter the crystal directly, will be deflected to be transformed into Light energy. Thus homes as well as personal energies will remain untouched.

The Hypothalamus (region of the brain controlling body temperature, thirst and hunger)

The hypothalamus is the central switchboard of our nervous system. Therefore, the crystal we have specifically programmed to accept positive thoughts, will receive only those. All other grey and harmful thought patterns will be blocked. By programming our crystal and using its ability as an amplifier, we are definitely communicating correctly. The hypothalamus, in turn, sends our message to every cell of our being, including our subconscious mind.

Our human body has a deep understanding and innate ability to decode every message received. The mind is a fine-tuner. However, we need an amplifier to bring the message into our conscious awareness. Quartz crystals are these amplifiers and become our greatest friends. Their clarity helps us to connect with our deepest truths. We begin to live in heightened awareness with daily practice.

We can even programme a crystal by holding it to the Third Eye (*Ajna* chakra). Focus intense intent onto the crystal in a balanced and quiet state of mind. The energy now passes through the crystal and harmonises within. It is extremely important to preserve this harmony.

Ideally, a crystal should be worn touching the Heart or Solar Plexus chakra. These are the most sensitive centres for receiving energy. They are very important as they hold intuition and awareness. Therefore, a crystal touching these centres will always protect and enhance our energies.

Even if we feel that some extraneous energy has entered our crystal, we just hold it in the sun and place an intent that it is clear of holding all past memories of another person. When we hold our crystal, its energy starts flowing into us and ours starts flowing into it. This energy is amplified by the crystal and relayed through the nervous system, flowing up towards our arms and reaching the hypothalamus gland in the brain. This gland lines the emotional centre, the pleasure centre, the pituitary gland and the nervous system.

Always remember that a crystal repeats its programming continuously. Therefore, all our intentions are constantly in an active state in the present moment even when we are absorbed in our daily routine. It is like giving all our major responsibilities to a trusted friend who is working on them at every moment. This is so wonderful to observe and experience.

To erase its previous programming and feed in a new one, we first hold the crystal in our active palm, face the Sun, and request that it should completely erase the crystal's earlier memory. The crystal is now ready for a new programme. The ease of working with crystals actually helps us to understand how simple we can be in our lives. We can undo the complex thought patterns of the mind and relax in the simplicity of the good that is our innate nature.

When we wish to give a gift of a crystal, we should programme it with powerful visualisation. Visualise that the person is within the crystal, enjoying perfect health and balance. Now charge this crystal with prayer for several days before giving it away. It will have merged its energies with the Divine. Let your friend know what the programme is so that they may change it if they wish.

We can programme and activate generator crystals for world peace and unity. Place the intent thus: "The infinite power of the universe has gathered itself to create a true and grand harmony."

We can programme our generator crystal for manifesting specific needs. We place our written affirmation with a picture (a new home, a fine job, a loving partner, higher education) and put the generator over it with our intent. Remember, if it is for our good in the larger picture, it will return to us multiplied.

CHAPTER 8

HEALING WITH CRYSTALS

CHAKRAS

Chakra means 'spinning wheel' in Sanskrit. The wheel represents the degree of energy in an individual's body. These chakras are also called Lotuses and are the receivers and transmitters of energy.

Just as a lotus blooms on the water despite its roots being buried deep in the muddy pond, similarly the chakra can open and blossom in the Divine Light even though it is rooted in our physical self. We become lotuses which are *in* the world but not tainted *by* it.

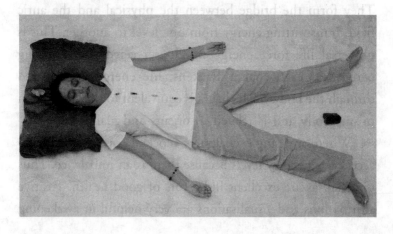

Chakra	Organ	Gland
Muladhara (Base)	Large intestine, Rectum, Kidneys.	Adrenal
Svadhisthana (Sacral)	Reproductive system, Bladder, Kidneys.	Testes, Ovaries.
Manipura (Solar Plexus)	Liver, Gall bladder, Stomach, Spleen, Small intestine.	Pancreas
Anahata (Heart)	Heart, Arms.	Thymus
Vishuddhi (Throat)	Lungs, Throat.	Thyroid, Parathyroid.
Ajna (Brow)	Brain.	Pituitary
Sahasrara (Crown)	Whole being.	Pineal
Spirit	Whole being.	All

Chakras are found in our subtle body, which is our aura. They form the bridge between the physical and the auric field, transmitting energy from one level to another. This is universal life force energy which is received by all living beings. As each chakra awakens, life energy is regulated through the body. Each chakra is equivalent to a major system in our body and is related to organs and glands.

When any single chakra is blocked, one is unable to access one's energy levels because there is an imbalance. Thus the chakras are excellent indicators of good health. Positive affirmations and visualisations are very helpful in awakening the chakras. The main chakras have rainbow colours which indicate their vibratory levels. There is a sound vibration for each chakra and it is known as *beej* mantra (the seed sound) in Sanskrit.

True healing happens when all chakras are cleared. All other healing amounts to a suppression of the root cause. When chakras are balanced, an inner harmony rises because the root cause has been cleared. This is vital for wellness. The opening of all the chakras gives us clarity, confidence and spiritual guidance to remain centered and at peace with every breath we take without using anyone else as a crutch. One becomes independent.

OUR MAIN CHAKRAS

The main lower chakra is the *Muladhara* or Root chakra.

It is connected to the adrenal glands and represents stability. Its colour is a lush green like the sprawling grassy fields over Mother Earth.

This chakra grounds us with all living beings. When it blossoms, its energy rises in continuous upwards spirals through the other chakras and transforms them. This brings a sense of purpose, belonging and willingness to take responsibility for one's own thoughts, words and actions.

The one above the *Muladhara* is the Sacral Chakra or the *Hara*, which means 'seat of power' in Japanese. Its Sanskrit name is *Svadhisthana* meaning 'sweetness' or 'one's own abode'. It is located within the abdomen, midway between the pubic bone and the navel. It is connected with the ovaries/

testes. Its colour is a deep, bright orange like the blazing fire of the sun and it represents well-being and self-confidence.

This chakra must be cleared of past karma before energy can rise any higher. Man is only a transitional being living in a mental consciousness, but with full possibility of acquiring Truth consciousness and living a perfectly harmonious and balanced life. Ideas and desires which are born here stimulate the mind. It is when this chakra blossoms that there is an increase in intuition and psychic abilities. The sexual energy is used constructively, bringing completeness and oneness with the body. Sages in ancient civilisations gave all their time to establish within themselves the supramental energy by raising their sexual fluid energy and using it for spiritual progress.

The next main chakra is the Solar Plexus, located between the twelfth thoracic vertebra and the first lumbar vertebra. It is connected to the pancreas gland. Its colour is a deep yellow like a field of daffodils or sunflowers. It is called *Manipura* in Sanskrit which means 'city of jewels' and represents our true will, potential and power. This chakra stores universal life force energy which can be directed to any part of the body or to other people through visualisation. It is the central point of our power (our spiritual reality). When this chakra blossoms, we master the ability to see our body from within. When the Solar Plexus energies are blocked, people suppress their emotions, their drive and their anger. They function from fear and worry, and experience what is called 'butterflies in the stomach'. When this chakra is completely open, the person has self-determination and will-power.

The next main chakra is the Heart chakra, its Sanskrit name being *Anahata*, which means 'unstruck sound'. It is located between the fourth and fifth thoracic vertebrae at the centre of the chest. Its colour is deep red like lava flowing over our Earth, or pink, like millions of pink roses. It is connected with the thymus gland and deals with matters of the heart such as love, relationship and compassion.

It is not personal love but a universal unconditional love from our Heartlight to others. This unconditional love heals and changes situations when the chakras have been cleared of selfish, petty desires. Aspiration and selflessness now blossom. The ability to heal without discrimination and the ability to give and receive unconditionally is enhanced. Compassion becomes part of the person's nature.

The next main chakra is the Throat chakra. Its Sanskrit name is *Vishuddhi* which means 'purification through clearing toxins'. It is located at the throat and is linked to the thyroid and parathyroid gland. Its colour is bright blue like the clear sky stretching endlessly above us.

It symbolises clarity of voice, communicating and expressing feelings effectively and genuinely.

When this chakra is opened, it increases telepathy (inner hearing). Creativity becomes active and the awareness that our consciousness is eternal, now blossoms. This makes it much easier for us to understand our past, present and future.

The next main chakra is the Third Eye chakra. Its Sanskrit

name is *Ajna* which means 'to know' or 'to command'. It is linked to the pituitary master gland and is located between the eyebrows, just above the bridge of the nose. Its colour is a deep indigo.

This chakra mirrors the depth of our Heartlight. It is the *eye* of our Heartlight and increases sixth sense, perception, awareness, intuition, and brings freedom. It gets us in touch with our inner wisdom. (All the answers we seek outside are within us, we are our own teachers.)

Now comes the Crown. It is our Cap of Light and the foundation for our seventy-two spiritual chakras above. It is violet or pearlescent silver white in colour. The Sanskrit name for it is *Sahasrara* which means 'thousandfold'. It is connected to the pineal master gland and is located four fingers above the crown of the head. When this energy centre is opened, we experience union and bliss with the Divine.

When it begins to blossom, richer and deeper thoughts and emotions are experienced. The body enjoys good health. Mental focus is enhanced. Intuitiveness strengthens, and a direct link is forged between our Heartlight and the Divine Light and this gives us a feeling of having reached home.

The Crown opens up to seventy-two spiritual chakras. They are a brilliant white colour, signifying purity and peace. These chakras are twenty times the height of our body and connect us directly with our higher self at the seventy-second spiritual chakra level. It is our highest connection with the Divine Light.

When these chakras open and blossom, we are in a continuous state of heightened awareness of the Supramental force working within us. One is constantly functioning from spiritual rather than mental awareness. Therefore the qualities of peace, harmony, love, compassion, forgiveness, understanding, generosity, humility and gratitude form the person's consciousness. It is the spiritual umbilical cord connection which each soul enjoys in every birth.

Chakra	Function	Malfunction
Root	Survival, grounding.	Obesity, haemorrhoids, constipation, sciatica.
Hara	Pleasure, sexuality, procreation, creativity.	Impotence, frigidity, uterine, bladder, kidney.
Solar Plexus	Will and power.	Ulcers, diabetes, eating disorders.
Heart	Love	Asthma, blood pressure, lung and heart disease.
Throat	Creativity, communication.	Sore throat, swollen glands, colds, thyroid.
Third Eye	Direct perception.	Headaches, nightmares, defects of vision.
Crown	Union with the Divine.	Alienation
Spiritual	Endless Light.	Resentment, ingratitude, ego.

Human chart showing placement of chakras

Chakra	Colour	Beej mantra (Seed Sound)
72 SPIRITUAL CENTRES	Pearlescent silver white	Hrih
CROWN	Pearlescent silver/Violet	A'ha
THIRD EYE	Indigo	A'hu
THROAT	Blue	Hum
HEART	Red/pink	Yum
SOLAR PLEXUS	Yellow	Rum
SACRAL	Orange	Vum
BASE	Green	Lum

Chakra	Colour	Beej mantra
72 Spiritual Centres	Pearlescent silver white	Hrih
Crown	Pearlescent silver/Violet	A'ha
Third Eye	Indigo	A'hu
Throat	Blue	Hum
Heart	Red/Pink	Yum
Solar Plexus	Yellow	Rum
Sacral	Orange	Vum
Base	Green	Lum

THE HUMAN AURA

Our physical body is surrounded by a sheath called the aura which is actually energy.

The innermost layer is the etheric body, which is a glow generated by living cells. All the diseases first appear in this etheric field. We can discover our etheric field by cupping our hands together and visualising a ball in the centre. Slowly move the palms, as though you are rotating a ball. You will feel a magnetic force between them (Pics. 1 and 2 overleaf).

The astral field is the middle layer of the aura which reflects the emotional nature and feelings about relationships and situations.

The outer layer of the aura is the mental field. When higher mental faculties develop, this band of energy reflects inspiration and intuition.

AURA CLEANSING

It is essential to do a daily cleansing of the auric field. Cup your palms a foot apart, in front of your Heart chakra (Pic. 3 overleaf), and stand erect with your feet slightly apart. Like the wipers of a car, now take your palms above your crown, facing your body and criss-cross the action from the crown of your head to the tips of your toes without bending. When a person bends down, the auric field gets disturbed, so it is advisable to visualise that you are clearing the lower half of your body without bending. Do three sets of twelve each for the front, the sides and the back of the body (Pics. 4, 5, 6, 7 overleaf).

Fig. 1

Fig. 2

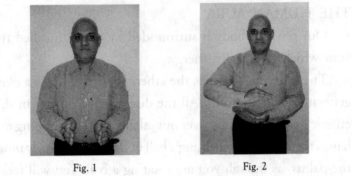

Fig. 3

Fig. 4

Fig. 5

Fig. 6

Fig. 7

CHANTING THE *BEEJ* MANTRA (seed sound)

After every aura clearing, it is highly recommended to chant the *beej* mantra for the chakras to remain in harmony. Refer to the chakra chart for each *beej* mantra.

We cup our palms over each specific chakra, visualise its individual colour and then intone its *beej* mantra in multiples of twelve. For instance, if we are experiencing a sore throat, we visualise the colour blue in that region and intone 'Hum' twelve times. As we do this five times each day for three days, we will definitely experience a wonderful clearing.

Crystal healings and meditations are extremely helpful to first clear all the built-up fatigue in the cellular structure. The body energy system tends to break down under stress and the powerful resonance of crystalline energy clarifies and reinstates inner balance. Our chakras receive an opening for Light and harmony.

Visualise being seated within a large and beautiful rose quartz pyramid. Holding a clear quartz generator in our active palm, and a rose quartz generator in the other palm, we keep the eyes closed and spine erect. Fill the pyramid with White Light. We are now in a healing chamber to receive the highest vibrational frequencies.

Visualise the Root chakra energies releasing all the grey of the past and receiving the White Light. The chakra petals will completely unfold and turn upwards. See the colour green and chant the Seed sound of this chakra – Lum.

You will likely wonder why the Root chakra is green,

when you have previously read or heard that it is red. The explanation for this is when God created man in His image, He breathed His life breath into man. The original eight red blood cells of Divine love were thus activated in man's heart. God must have had the aspiration that man will raise his vibratory frequencies and his higher chakras will remain open to sustain his relationship with God, and that there would be a wonderful relationship together. I am sure of this.

However, man's energy frequencies went into downwards spirals from the beginning of time, through succumbing to temptation. The Divine love cells of bright red sank into the lower chakras and came to rest at the base of the spine. We know the spine as the Staff of God.

This Divine energy coiled and remained stifled and stuck at this point, dislodging the fresh, creative green energy colour of the Root. This colour, therefore, had to find room in the empty space of the Heart centre. It is when we receive cosmic attunements and other healing frequencies that this red colour once again finds an opening to enter the Heart and we grow in willingness to accept change. Above all we are open to release the greatest insanity – the lodged enemy of doubt that breeds fear.

Now, we raise our consciousness to our Sacral chakra. The colour is orange and the Seed sound to heal this chakra is Vum. We repeat the same process as we keep focusing our attention on each chakra till we reach our Cap of Light – the Crown.

The Solar Plexus chakra is golden yellow and the Seed sound is Rum.

The Heart chakra holds the essence of the original red blood cells of Divine love and the Seed sound is Yum.

The Throat chakra is the colour blue as of the sky and the Seed sound is Hum.

The Third Eye chakra is indigo and the Seed sound is A'hu. This is the sound of the breath of God which began all creation. This sound is that word.

The Crown is violet/pearlescent silver white and the Seed sound is A'ha. This is the sound frequency which expands our consciousness and carries us into the Super Mind.

The seventy-two higher spiritual chakras are pearlescent silver and the Seed sound is Hrih. This vibratory frequency connects us to the One God.

We allow our entire being to feel the new energies within the White Light of the rose pyramid. Now we will very likely be able to move into our clear quartz crystal. Here we receive the healing for clarity and confidence (two minutes). We will probably be seeing the colours of our chakras in this state of quietude.

We are now ready to seal the energies received. Visualise each chakra closing its petals, enclosing the protective energies for ourselves. Start with the Cap of Light, the Crown, and close with the Root. Our amplifier and receiver energies are now finally tuned. Doing this meditation exercise daily makes it a part of our life.

HEALING WITH CRYSTALLINE ENERGY

The secret for healing ourselves is to be in a constant flow of surrender and gratitude. We need to humbly acknowledge the Light and allow it to clear the blocks that keep us from our spirit truth.

We need to consciously reprogramme our thought patterns daily. It is a silent inner practice, which goes on simultaneously with our outer life. It flows continually with our inner awareness and becomes an integral flow.

Daily quiet time with a crystal meditation, affirmations and positive visualisation for at least twenty minutes is essential. We need to train our minds to focus on our inner Light essence so that our cells open up to receive the vibratory force.

Our physical bodies need a daily walk and a workout to clear stress and oxygenate the cells. The water energy in our body needs to flow rather than stagnate with a sedentary job. Body movement is as important as a healthy and nutritious diet. It is this that gives our emotional centre renewed hope and trust as a daily offering. We learn to love ourselves more than we can imagine.

As we create happy time spent alone for this daily work, we will experience a great inner peace filling us. Our gratitude expands, and our perspectives shift, leading to more forgiveness, compassion and joy. Fear and worry will be replaced with trust in Divine Order.

It is important to maintain and recharge this flow until it becomes a part of our new cell patterns and is ingrained in our psyche, one day at a time, listening to our intuition. This is the experience of a grounded ascension with crystal healing.

Like a laser beam, a crystal generates tremendous force and amplifies it for healing. We can hold our clear quartz double-pointed crystal near the source of pain and notice the healing happening. We can also rotate the crystal clockwise twelve times in the aura and then flick out the dense energies it has absorbed into the Violet Light, to be transmuted into White Light. Placed in the palms and at the soles of the feet, crystals help to clear many blockages. This is because there are scores of acupressure points on the palms and the soles which respond to the properties inherent in crystals.

The rational mind should best be quiet. Just listen to the intuitive voice. A harmonious mind channels harmony into the crystal which amplifies the message and programmes healing. A quartz crystal greatly amplifies the brain's ability to influence mind over matter. Once we understand the power of positive thoughts, we can train our minds on how to consciously change our thoughts and our lives.

Healing 1
Lie down comfortably on a bed or on the floor. Place a clear quartz double-pointed crystal on the Third Eye. It will produce a powerful effect of continuously drawing up physical energy and the auric field energy.

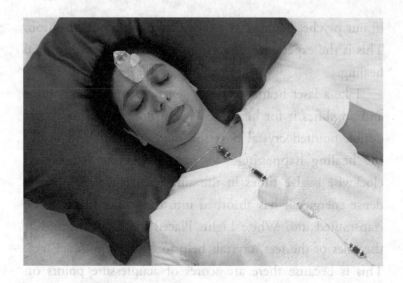

Be very relaxed and take ten deep, long, breaths. Keep the eyes closed and visualise being in a cocoon of the highest White Light.

Say a sincere prayer of gratitude:

"I thank the Divine Light for being present. I thank my own inner Light for being open and receptive. I come from a place of deep humility and I surrender, requesting a complete healing of my chakras."

Now, we become aware of the double-pointed crystal on our Third Eye and focus our entire attention on this crystal.

We visualise each of our chakras awakening, one at a time, from the Root to the Cap of Light.

We keep relaxed and notice if there are any colours or images that show up on the screen before our Third Eye, being in this state for twenty minutes. It is now time to seal the energy received in each chakra. Visualise each one sealing and be in gratitude. Gently removing the crystal, we turn on the right side and experience the warmth of being in our mother's womb. We take three deep long breaths, feeling the energy of protective Light enfolding our entire body. Now, we take the support of our left palm and rise, saying a prayer of gratitude.

Healing 2

This healing treatment can be done with partners. We visualise ourselves bathed in White Light. One person lies down comfortably and the other holds the clear quartz double-pointed crystal in the active hand, and the rose quartz in the other. The rose quartz is always pointed towards the Heart chakra, lending divine support to the person who channels the healing.

The clear quartz is held horizontally with one of its points facing towards the patient. It is slowly directed

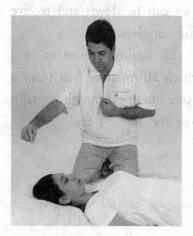

from the Crown on the person's right side and downwards to the toes. This is done by visualising the energy flowing through the lower body to the toes. There will be moments when the crystal voluntarily stops at a certain region of the body. It has picked up a block which needs to clear. Rotate the crystal twelve times clockwise and flick the dense energies it has absorbed into the Violet Light so that it is transformed into White Light, saying, "I offer all the mis-qualified energies into the Violet Light to be transmuted into White Light. Thank you."

We may have to repeat this procedure until the crystal voluntarily moves on from that region. Continue the flow till the tips of the toes and then change hands to facilitate the crystal healing. We now come up to the Crown on the left side of the body. We have just completed an elliptical circuit of healing. We always conclude with a prayer of gratitude and blow the life breath into our crystals with love. We now wash them and programme them for the next partner's session. Now we can lie down and receive the same energy treatment for ourselves.

Be creative. We can give this healing treatment to a photograph, or even to a written affirmation. Just place a clear quartz crystal with a sincere intent on the photograph or affirmation and then follow the above steps.

CHAPTER 9

UNDERSTANDING THE CHAKRA CIRCUIT

'Chakra' is Sanskrit for a spinning wheel.

Chakras are spinning vortices that focus certain vibratory frequencies of energy. Each time we accumulate stress, our chakra field is less able to assimilate and direct the cosmic energy into our being. We feel tired and listless. When a specific chakra is experiencing pain, the surrounding chakras will come to its aid and spend their energy to heal it. Over time this often contributes to an ailment or emotional imbalance. The strain is apparent. Each chakra, or energy centre as it is called, is linked to a physical function as well as emotional and mental functions. Each main chakra has a healing Seed sound as well as a healing colour to soothe the energy into wellness.

For this healing we require the crystals associated with the colours of each chakra.

For instance, we must place amethyst crystals around the head and shoulders. If we are using single-pointed generators, they should be pointed downwards.

On the throat, we place a blue stone – lapis lazuli, aquamarine or turquoise.

For the heart, we use a bloodstone, ruby, garnet or rose quartz.

Place a yellow agate or citrine on the solar plexus.

For the sacral, use an orange carnelian.

The root can have a green jade, green quartz, kyanite or malachite.

At the feet, place a black tourmaline.

We can use A Grade therapeutic essential oils to enhance cell renewal and balance.

Take five long, deep breaths and feel completely relaxed. Be in gratitude and visualise the great White Light descending. For the next twenty minutes (set your biological clock or use an alarm clock), just be aware of the flow of breath and let the crystalline energy work through each chakra, piercing through the veils with dazzling positive frequencies. We then open our eyes with a prayer of sincere gratitude, feeling refreshed and light. Sometimes, several

MAIN CHAKRAS IN THE BODY

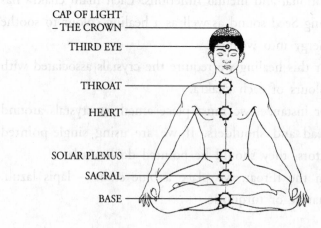

CAP OF LIGHT – THE CROWN

THIRD EYE

THROAT

HEART

SOLAR PLEXUS

SACRAL

BASE

layers of old stagnant energy release, leaving us with a feeling of nausea. Use the next two hours to relax and be calm. Each healing experience continues to flow through our system for the next five hours. It is advisable to maintain a relaxed state after a session.

CHAKRA BALANCING

It is important for every Light worker to understand the chakra energy field. Chakras hold spiritual energy and occur where nerve endings come together. These are the pressure points and psychic centres of our vital force. They are interconnected with all the body systems, so the physical body is connected to the chakras. Each chakra is connected to the spine, right from the Root chakra upwards, drawing energy from the auric field. This is then distributed through the corresponding gland in the physical body.

The energy appears like currents or waves with the most beautiful colours. In spiritually developed people, the chakras pulsate with glowing Light energy. Such people have more energy and vigour than others and are therefore better able to accomplish their goals. The chakras are constantly rotating and releasing energy which saturates the body cells.

At birth, every baby has chakras which are completely vibrant and open. However, because of our environment, culture and upbringing, our chakras get blocked and imbalanced. Thus, the basic life force slows down within the individual. Low feelings, depression, fear, worry, and mood swings set in early in life.

On the other hand, those who sustain their daily inner practice have chakras which are open and receptive to wholesome life force energy.

Crystals are extremely effective healers because they are related to us in many ways. They contain seventy per cent water, just like we do. They are also made up of the five elements, like us. Hence, we can make an immediate connection with crystalline energy. Crystalline vibrations stimulate a sluggish chakra energy field and bring balance.

THE ROOT CHAKRA
MULADHARA – (the reliability of a strong root)

This chakra is located at the base of the spine and holds the survival instinct in man. It is the lowest among the main chakras in a human being and the highest in an animal. It helps ground the person when there is harmony in every cell.

When blocked, the person has doubts, fears, anxiety, anger and stress. The bodily imbalances related to this chakra are constipation, arthritis, nervousness, poor digestion, cartilage injury, knee problems and sciatica.

Calmness and wisdom denote a grounded person. It is linked to the adrenal glands.

Visualise the colour green and use the green jade with the Seed sound, Lum.

THE SACRAL CHAKRA
SVADHISHTHANA – (to be in one's own place)

This chakra is located just below the navel and is the home of desires, pleasures, procreation and sexuality. A blocked Sacral chakra holds a frigid and restless nature. The person can be confused, impotent, and may have lower back pain along with kidney ailments.

For those whose Sacral chakra is open and receptive, the emotions are strong and confident. The person is full of courage and aware of the power within. Visualise the colour orange and use the orange carnelian with the Seed sound, Vum.

It is linked to the gonads.

THE SOLAR PLEXUS CHAKRA
MANIPURA – (the city of jewels)

This chakra is above the navel along the eighth thoracic vertebra.

It develops the healthy ego which assists us in our goals, warm feelings, balanced emotions, strong will power, and keen knowledge. Such a person is always in the right place at the right time and in the power of the present moment. Charitable and selfless, the person exudes harmony in every situation. Material importance is of little consequence.

Visualise a golden yellow colour and use the yellow agate or a citrine with the Seed sound, Rum.

It is linked to the pancreas and spleen.

THE HEART CHAKRA
ANAHATA – (the unstruck sound)

This chakra is at the centre of the heart region and is connected with love. It is a chakra which is difficult to open but once it begins release, the tap flows and all the body chakras can align with it since the heart is connected to the entire body through the circulatory system.

A blocked Heart chakra brings on blood pressure, heart ailments, asthma, and lung diseases.

A balanced Heart chakra opens us to love, gentle understanding, compassion, tenderness and a complete ability to respond with love in every relationship and situation.

Visualise the colour red or pink and use the bloodstone, garnet, ruby or rose quartz with the Seed sound, Yum.

It is linked to the heart and thymus gland.

THE THROAT CHAKRA
VISHUDDHI – (cleansing the poison with purity of intent)

This chakra is located at the base of the throat along the third cervical vertebra. It deals with the higher self, creativity and communicative ability. This is the centre where our body, mind, emotions, feelings and spirit raise their combined clarity to move into good thoughts, good words and good action. It is where we begin to awaken in life.

A blocked Throat chakra brings rigid points of view, clogged communication channels, coughs and colds, a stiff neck and hearing problems; whereas a balanced one brings confidence, calmness and the understanding of the Highest Light and good living.

Visualise the colour blue as of the sky and use the turquoise, aquamarine or lapis lazuli with the Seed sound, Hum.

It is linked to the thyroid gland.

THE THIRD EYE CHAKRA
AJNA – (the command centre)

This chakra is located in the middle of the forehead, between the eyebrows along the first cervical vertebra.

It is the command centre which brings clarity, intuition and clairvoyance.

A blocked Third Eye chakra results in headaches, nightmares, strained vision and even blindness.

Visualise the colour indigo and use the amethyst with the Seed sound, A'hu.

It is linked to the pineal and pituitary glands.

THE CROWN
SAHASRARA – (a thousand-petalled lotus)

This grand lotus is located on the top of the head. It is our Cap of Light energy that connects us directly into our seventy-two spiritual chakras which merge with the Source. Therefore, it is called the Crown.

When blocked, the person is depressed, bored, confused and lonely.

On the other hand, a person who has an open energy here is always filled with love. Such a person flows with gentle healing words and thoughts, coupled with humility, obedience, willingness, and surrenders to a deep, understanding wisdom. This represents the highest divine bliss, while in the human body.

It is linked to the pineal and pituitary glands.

Visualise the colour violet or pearlescent silver, using the amethyst or clear quartz and the Seed sound, A'ha.

Now that we have understood the basic work of these main energy centres, we can use our double-pointed clear quartz crystal over each, to balance the energies. We will find the crystal moving smoothly from one chakra to another, where there is harmony. Wherever there is a resistance, gently rotate the crystal twelve times and flick the grey energies absorbed into it, out into the Violet Light to be transmuted into White Light as described earlier.

Crystals help to regulate the functions of our subtle bodies, which are the energy structures of each aspect of the self that interpenetrate and extend beyond our physical body. This field or space is what we are all aware of, when we feel or sense someone too close for our comfort, or conversely want to draw that special someone right into our space and hold them tight in our field. This is our aura – our auric field where energy interacts on many levels. Placing crystals within the auric field assists in maintaining the flow of energy information in a balanced way. Stagnant energy is released and the entire subtle body is realigned.

Closest to our physical body is the etheric body. It provides the blueprint for our body and its organs. This field always has a veil of imbalance before an ailment manifests in the physical. This is when we are known to say: "I feel like a body pain and fever coming on." And, the next thing is that we have a fever.

The emotional body is what we can feel distinctly from another. It virtually speaks to us with constantly changing emotions. This field is the easiest to clear with crystalline healing. All of us require this clearing at regular intervals.

The mental field contains our belief system and thought patterns. It heals when we do our inner work* along with crystal healing. This finer, subtle field holds within it our spiritual goals and aspirations. It holds our link to the collective unconscious as well as the link of awareness to the larger universal energy patterns.

All of these fields can be worked on with crystals and a deep core cleansing can happen.

---

* Inner work is our vigilant awareness level through the day as we go about our activities in situations and relationships. It is an intense constant practice of maintaining inner balance and harmony, of holding inner peace in the face of seeming disturbances and challenges.

CHAPTER 10

CRYSTALLINE GRID HEALING

A crystal grid is a configuration of certain stones which helps us to heal ourselves and our space.

Grids should be created after a week-long meditation so that our intense intent flows into our sacred aspiration. It is good to own an energised grid from a healer or crystal therapist. A sensitive and gifted healer can greatly support us to reach out and unfold our full potential with the help of a crystal grid. The grid is an extremely skilled work of divine art, which experienced therapists create through intent.

Health grids, peace and harmony grids, student con-centration grids, business success grids, relationship harmony grids, money multiplier grids, fertility grids, rid-the-evil-eye grids, abundance grids, fearlessness and confidence grids are some of the main ones we can use to transform our day-to-day lives.

Businessmen place spectacular crystal grids at manage-ment meetings for inspiration, focus and harmony during their sessions.

A crystal grid for the kitchen ensures freshness, creativity, inspiration and harmony.

A garden grid revives our plants, bringing abundant growth.

Cut flowers last much longer when tumbled crystalline stones are added to the water in the vase.

In the farmyard, a crystal grid wards off slugs and snails.

A grid for pets helps maintain good health and understanding. We can attach a tumbled black tourmaline stone to a dog collar for health and safety. Animals are keenly sensitive to crystalline energy and respond to it immediately.

To calm and quieten a pet's nature, we can place a double-pointed rose quartz by the feeding bowl or bed. We must ensure that the crystal is placed hidden or away from the pet's reach.

A crystal grid for abundance, or for peace and harmony, makes an excellent gift to dear friends on special occasions because it adds to the peace, love and joy in their lives. A grid is activated through intent energy programming done by an experienced Master.

A Peace and Harmony Grid (Pic. 104)

This grid is made of an assortment of rose quartz and clear quartz crystals in a glass bowl. Placing this grid in the living room encourages a sense of peace and well-being for everyone around.

An Abundance Grid (Pic. 102)

This grid is created by placing all the main chakra stones

in a glass bowl. The energies of all these stones attract abundance into our lives.

Once a grid is created, it must be activated with intense intent. For this, it is best to attend a crystal grid workshop, so that we learn how to create our own grids and even start our own practice.

The Fearlessness Grid (Pic. 103)

This grid is made of a flawless, clear quartz cube with fifty-four powerful pyramids that clear all fear of situations and relationships from the mind of a person. Place this grid over the picture of the person who needs healing. Ideally, it should be kept on a bedside table.

CHAPTER 11

CRYSTAL HEALING WITH ESSENTIAL OILS

It is a wonderful art to combine crystalline energy with the energy of A Grade therapeutic essential oils.

Essential oils have been man's most ancient medicine. They oxygenate the body cells and revive them bringing balance. When a single oil's fragrance is inhaled, the amygdala in the limbic system of the brain plays a major role. It assists in the storing and releasing of emotional trauma. It can only be stimulated with the sense of smell. It responds to the fragrance by sending the message to the specific body cells which need oxygenation. Within minutes, a headache is relieved, fatigue is released, fevers come down, the entire immune system recharges and much more happens.

When pure oils are used with crystals, we definitely see a quantum leap in the healing session. For instance, soak tired feet in a large bowl of assorted chakra stones with two drops of lavender oil in warm water. Allow the healing energies to release all the fatigue for ten minutes.

Another good example is to soak our feet similarly in eucalyptus oil coupled with turquoise for a throat infection.

All the reflexology points in the soles of our feet receive immediate release and relaxation.

I find this combination of crystals with oils great fun! Encouraging feedback from my clients and patients keeps me in creative mode all the time.

Wearing rose oil with the rose quartz stone is excellent for all-round clearing of mental weariness and stress, and to enhance relaxation.

Wearing lavender with the amethyst is a relaxant for all fatigue – emotional, mental and physical.

Basil, cypress and peppermint oils with green aventurine or jade are useful for structural alignment to release the imbalance of the past.

Helichrysum with clear quartz unites the head and heart for clarity and confidence. This is an extremely valuable combination for the times we live in.

Bergamot with star ruby or rose quartz opens a closed heart.

Frankincense with amethyst opens the Third Eye to assist in awakening to Spirit self.

There is immense wealth awaiting us when we awaken to this joy.

CHAPTER 12

THE SRI YANTRA

The Sri Yantra is sacred geometry, which is imbued with the qualities of divine fulfilment. 'Sri' is a title given in India, for high respect – for one who is daily connected with the Divine, drawing upon the highest insight and power and who can therefore fulfil all aspirations. 'Yantra' refers to a mechanism.

The Sri Yantra is a divine storehouse of energy which picks up cosmic waves and transforms them into constructive vibrations which transmit into the atmosphere. Therefore, the Sri Yantra destroys all negative forces in its vicinity. Science has acknowledged its constructive cosmic concept.

Having infinite power of absorption and reflection of energies, it is heralded as the most powerful yantra in the Indian epics, symbolic of the Divine male and female energies together. It is the most powerful yantra for wisdom and abundance, and is said to remove all obstacles in our life and in our world.

Through its shape (it has many circles, triangles, points, lines and angles within) the complete life cycle in the universe is re-created. It neutralises negative planetary effects and brings immense good fortune to the owner.

It is best to place this intricately beautiful clear quartz structure in our prayer space or crystal altar.

Energise it daily by holding it under running water. We hold it in our active hand and visualise our goal with intense intent.

Now we place it in a glass bowl of water during prayer or meditation, and light fragrant incense sticks. A candle and flowers add to clearing the room energy.

We drink the water once we are done. We ingest our intent and as it is digested in our cellular energy, it manifests in our life.

To enable the highest energies to manifest in our world, have the Sri Yantra cleansed and programmed by an experienced healer or crystal therapist.

Sri Yantra

CHAPTER 13

ENVIRONMENTAL PLACEMENT OF CRYSTALS

Crystals reduce the effects of mental and emotional burdens. Electromagnetic pollution is also checked by placing crystals in those specific areas. They absorb the imbalance very effectively.

A rose quartz heart or rock crystal in the bedroom brings in positive energy.

A black tourmaline or a clear quartz cluster placed beside electrical gadgets and wiring neutralises the harmful effects. The same can be placed securely in the car to reduce fatigue and enhance focus especially at night.

A black tourmaline or amethyst rock by the telephone helps in reducing emotional involvement in telephone conversations.

The same rocks can be placed in bathrooms to clear the energies and maintain a refreshing flow of vibrations.

Green quartz in the kitchen adds to inspirational cooking.

Clear and rose quartz on the study table brings clarity and fearlessness in students.

Clear quartz and rose quartz crystals placed in a jug of water help balance the body energies and attract abundance.

Wearing crystal pendants, rings, bracelets and earrings all help to maintain the body energy levels.

Plant energy as well as pet energy is enhanced with the use of crystals. There is grounding, harmonising and calming.

CHAPTER 14

BIRTHSTONES FOR
EACH MONTH

Birthstones are associated with the Zodiac signs, as well as with what month we are born in. The origin of the twelve birthstones for the twelve months of the calendar is believed to have been the breastplate of Aaron, the Jewish High Priest, who was also the brother of Moses. (Exodus 28, 15-30)

The difference between the monthly and the Zodiac stones is that the monthly stones have more of a numerological association whereas the Zodiac stones relate more to astrology.

January – The glittering red garnet is the stone representing January in Hebrew, Roman, Arabic, Polish and Russian traditions.

February – The symbolic stone is the amethyst according to North American, Hebrew, Roman, Arabic, Polish and Russian traditions.

March – Modern North American culture names the aquamarine as the stone for this month. However, in Hebrew, Roman, Arabic, Polish and Russian traditions, it is the bloodstone.

April – North American culture names the diamond as the birthstone. In Jewish, Hindu and Polish cultures the diamond is also named as the April birthstone. However in Roman, Persian and Russian traditions, the stone is sapphire.

May – In contemporary North American, Arabic, Hindu, Polish and Russian traditions, the birthstone is emerald. However, the Hebrew and Roman traditions say it is agate.

June – June is one of those months that seems to be symbolised by an array of stones. Contemporary North American culture names the moonstone, pearl or alexandrite. Ancient Hindu tradition also names the pearl. However, in ancient Roman and Hebrew traditions June was ruled by the emerald, possibly because the green represented summer. In Russian, Polish and Arabic cultures, the stone is agate which comes in many colours.

July – In North American, Polish and Russian culture the birthstone is ruby. In Hebrew and Roman traditions it is onyx. The Arabic culture assigns the carnelian and the Hindu religion names the sapphire.

August – The modern North American tradition says peridot. The Hebrew and Roman traditions attribute it to the carnelian. The Arabic and Polish traditions say sardonyx. The Hindu tradition assigns the ruby and the Russian tradition, the alexandrite.

September – In modern North American traditions, it is the sapphire. However in Hebrew, Roman, Arabic, Polish and Russian traditions it is peridot. The Hindu tradition assigns the zircon.

October – The opal or the tourmaline is assigned to October. However, Hebrew, Roman, Arabic and Polish birth gemstone traditions say aquamarine. The Russian culture says beryl. Ancient Hindu tradition says coral.

November – The North American tradition assigns yellow topaz or citrine. The Hebrew, Roman, Arabic and Russian traditions also say topaz. The Hindu culture says cat's eye.

December – The North American tradition says three blue stones: tanzanite, turquoise or blue topaz. The Hindu religion also assigns it to topaz, and the Russian and Polish traditions assign it to turquoise. The Arabic, Roman and Hebrew traditions say the rose coloured ruby.

This is interesting because very often our choice of a Zodiac stone will conflict with the birth month stone. Some of the stones also cross over to astrology. For instance, if you are born in November the symbolic stone is topaz and if you are a Sagittarian born after the 23rd of November, then your stone will be a topaz as well.

Birthstones that match Zodiac signs

	Zodiac Sign	Stones
	Aries – Ram (Mar. 20 - Apr. 19)	Bloodstone, Carnelian, Jasper, Coral, Aquamarine, Emerald, Ruby, Diamond.
	Taurus – Bull (Apr. 19 - May 20)	Rose Quartz, Tiger's Eye, Topaz, Lapis Lazuli, Emerald, Diamond.
	Gemini – Twins (May 20 - Jun. 21)	Agate, Moonstone, Pearl, Citrine, Emerald.
	Cancer – Crab (Jun. 21 - Jul. 22)	Moonstone, Pearl, Ruby, Emerald, Amber.
	Leo – Lion (Jul. 22 - Aug. 23)	Topaz, Onyz, Cat's Eye, Ruby, Clear Quartz, Emerald.
	Virgo – Virgin (Aug. 23 - Sept. 22)	Moonstone, Sapphire, Peridot, Opal, Carnelian.
	Libra – Scales (Sept. 22 - Oct. 23)	Opal, Tourmaline, Jade, Lapis Lazuli, Emerald, Aventurine, Sapphire, Blue Lace Agate.
	Scorpio – Scorpion (Oct. 23 - Nov. 22)	Dark Opal, Aquamarine, Turquoise, Garnet, Topaz.
	Sagittarius – Archer (Nov. 22 - Dec. 21)	Topaz, Turquoise, Amethyst, Malachite, Lapis Lazuli.
	Capricorn – Goat (Dec. 21 - Jan. 20)	Turquoise, Diamond, Onyx, Ruby, Garnet, Clear Quartz.
	Aquarius – Water Bearer (Jan. 20 - Feb. 18)	Amethyst, Aquamarine, Jade, Diamond, Onyx, Ruby, Garnet, Turquoise, Sapphire.
	Pisces – Fish (Feb. 18 - Mar. 20)	Aquamarine, Amethyst, Bloodstone, Tourmaline, Pearl, Rose Quartz, Turquoise.

Note: There are several dates used for the zodiac. This is the chart the author uses for her classification.

How birthstones affect the body, mind and spirit

Colours	Anatomy	Meditation	Keyword
Red, White	Head, Face.	I actively pursue the fulfilment of my desires.	Initiative
Green	Throat, Neck.	I lovingly safeguard my environment.	Conservation
Yellow, Orange	Hands, Arms, Shoulders, Lungs, Nervous system.	My mind is linked to the Divine Source.	Versatility
Silver, Pearl, White	Stomach, Breasts.	I am in touch with my inner feelings.	Receptivity
Gold, Scarlet	Heart, Upper back.	I express love through service.	Magnetic
Grey, Navy	Abdomen, Intestines, Gall bladder.	My energy glows with light from the source.	Discriminate
Blues, Pink	Appendix, Kidney, Lower back.	I am creating bravery and harmony.	Harmony
Burgundy	Reproductive system.	I achieve mastery through transformation.	Intensity
Royal Blue, Purple	Hips, Thighs, Sciatic nerves.	All things are in harmony with the highest law.	Optimism
Black	Skeleton, Knees, Skin.	I am mastering the challenge of the physical plane.	Structure
Glowing Blue, Violet	Ankles, Circulatory system.	I create new paths by focussing my mind.	Unconventional
Violet, Sea Green	Feet, Lymphatic system.	I surrender to the heart of Divine Compassion.	Transcendental

CHAPTER 15

MANIFESTATION IN ACTION

Wonderful things happen when working with crystals. Our limited minds often have no explanation for what takes place. Here, I would like to share with you the incredible experience I have had with my channeling crystal.

This beautiful Transmitter has been among my first crystals.

Its place is on my crystal altar and, ten years ago, my friend picked it up from my table where I had kept it to be packed, as I was travelling that evening. She said, "Any way I look at it, I see a guardian spirit in your crystal." I was quite amazed, and had a look myself. She was right! I was very excited and extremely grateful.

The next year, I was on a visit to Sri Ramana Maharshi's Ashram at Tiruvannamalai in South India, and once again I took all my crystals with me. The experience in Tiruvannamalai was beautiful, especially discovering that the Arunachala Mountain is full of clear quartz crystal energy!

My friends took me to visit an extremely devout lady called Amma. It was an amazing experience to be with her, and we became very close friends. I was at that time guided by immense love to give her my channeling crystal, which I did. I explained to her how to cleanse it and how it would enhance her energy.

I returned to Mumbai a week later and would often think of my channeling crystal with a lot of love, and mentally bless both Amma and the crystal I had given to her. A month later, I suddenly experienced an afternoon of immense loss. My crystal was calling out and the mother-child connection was tugging. This experience happened three more times. I opened up to the Universal guidance and received the clear message to request Amma to send me the crystal with anyone who was coming to Mumbai and I would send her a bloodstone generator. I wrote. Our letters crossed. She wrote saying that she had been unable to cleanse the crystal, hence she was guided to take it up with her to the Arunachala mountain, where she placed it in the ground (among its own kind!) for a couple of days, and when she received the message that it had been lovingly cleansed and recharged, she covered it with the beautiful, fragrant mud and lemon grass of the mountain, wrapped it up and sent it to me.

Just as I was concluding a weekend seminar in Mumbai, the doorbell rang, and I was delighted to see Darius, who had returned from Tiruvannamalai. He handed me this fragrant bundle, and words fail to describe how wonderful it was to be with my crystal once again. Amma wrote, "Gulrukh, your crystal kept itself here, to be healed and recharged. That is exactly what has happened, and now it's coming back to its owner."

This entire incident taught me yet again that it is possible for us and all other living beings (crystals) to be on a high consciousness level and link wherever we put our minds. We can all be connected with the Highest Good at all times. We have only to draw upon this reality and create daily fulfilment, which we call miracles.

CHAPTER 16

CASE STUDIES

The following case studies are good examples of how gratitude peacefully shifts realities, happening ever so surely with waves of Light.

As we begin to read this chapter, let us introspect and explore the vibratory frequency of the word 'gratitude'. It opens a deep awareness within us. Watch how our grateful spirit touches others and how their intense intentions open the floodgates of energy which flow into us. It is an awakening, a call for alert awareness.

Now read and watch how it manifests.

Case Study 1

Sheila came for crystal healing in 1999 with complaints of a highly stressful job as a computer engineer. She needed rejuvenation on a daily basis.

She learned crystal therapy and became a daily practitioner. This is what she did on herself: as soon as she got home from work, she relaxed with her single-pointed clear quartz generator, pointing outwards in her active hand and her single-pointed rose quartz generator pointing towards her heart in the other hand. This was her twenty-minute routine which directed energy from the universal Light field and distributed it throughout her energy field. She consciously visualised the energy flowing through her, revitalising her cells. It made a remarkable difference to her evenings. She felt so energised that the next three hours were peaceful and happy ones with her family.

Case Study 2

Prakash Mehra often complained of rheumatic pain when he first came for healing sessions in the year 2000. His wife suffered severe menstrual cramps. They had also got along a family friend who had arthritic pain in his knee and a sprained ankle as well. The following sequence helped each one to relieve their pain:

A single-pointed kyanite or a black star was placed with the point directed towards the specific area of complaint. For the next ten minutes they powerfully visualised that area receiving White Light. They also visualised that the pain had completely gone, while I simultaneously used a double-pointed clear quartz crystal, rotating it over the region, to clear the dense energy field. Three healing sessions later, they felt much better and were able to function without pain.

Case Study 3

Rajni and Meera are good friends who came for a consultation. Both felt exhaustion within hours of waking up.

They are housewives who constantly feel physically and mentally tired.

I advised them to lie down for twenty minutes and visualise an active, energising Light flowing through their cells. I placed amethyst pyramids on the Third Eye and Crown to clear the cellular energy. To open up their self-expression and communication, I placed aquamarine and turquoise on the throat. Rose quartz and bloodstone were placed on the heart for gentle, loving kindness towards themselves. On the Solar Plexus was placed the citrine for clear thinking and positivity. On the Sacral chakra I put an orange carnelian to enhance and empower their Light. On the Root, I placed a green jade and malachite to bring balance and self-worth. Twenty minutes later, I lifted the crystals and requested the ladies to turn on their right side and feel nurtured as if within their mothers' wombs. They arose feeling refreshed and vibrant. It was the highlight of my day.

Case Study 4

All case histories for headaches and migraines are helped by placing the kyanite and rose quartz stones on the specific problem area for ten minutes. Always remember that the back of the head is especially important for clearing stale emotional patterns, which are embedded in the subconscious. Coupled with powerful visualisation, this method works extremely well for relieving pain in other regions of the body too. Let us commit to actively reject all ailments, just as our mind rejects falsehood.

Experiences of Crystal Users

Case Study 1

On Tuesday, the 17th of July, 2001, I was travelling by public bus from Mumbai city to the suburbs. I was about to get down when suddenly the driver slammed the brakes to avoid a speeding autorickshaw. As a result, I was thrown a few feet away and my head and knee received severe injury. I was in extreme agony but was unable to do anything until I reached home. It was then that I used my single-pointed amethyst generator in spirals over the area of injury, while at the same time powerfully visualising the white Divine Light. I felt completely well in just ten minutes. I feel so grateful.

– Professor Shekhar R. Rege,
Siddharth College, Mumbai

Case Study 2

I was taken by complete surprise when I placed Dr. Bala's energised double-pointed clear quartz generator under my left arm intuitively. Within minutes, I felt a lot of metallic residue rising in my alimentary canal. It was old guck that tasted like poison in my mouth. It had obviously been loosened up for cleansing. This incident led me to attend Dr. Bala's workshop on crystal therapy. Two weeks into the treatment, I found so many of my questions being answered. I began to sleep more peacefully and found extra energy – almost seventy per cent more, for internal and external cleansing.

My home has had simultaneous constructive changes too. I understood that what we are inside manifests outside. I feel deeply grateful for the crystalline energy in my life.

On completing the Heartlight Ascension Level One workshop, I received my certificate in which Dr. Bala had written my maiden name! I was completely stunned. How did *she* know it? I asked her later, but she only smiled. I have kept the certificate as a very precious gift from the Divine.

– Anju Kohli

Case Study 3

Crystalline energy has shaped my inner awareness and steadily awakened me to my own divinity. It has been a difficult process, but the grace of the energy and the unstinted efforts of love and understanding provided by Dr. Gulrukh Bala have made the path so much clearer. Crystalline healing has helped me unveil, shed and let go. I have become a whole new person with more focused action, greater understanding and patience. I can deal with uncomfortable situations in a better way, heal my physical ailments and uplift the energies of those around me. My external life has merged with my inner Light and I feel lighter and happier. My emotions are in balance and every day I awaken in gratitude for the crystalline energies I work with.

– Minal Mehta

Case Study 4

I first met Dr. Gulrukh Bala when I contacted her for a crystalline therapy workshop in 2000. I had hardly ever imagined that such a workshop could be so enriching and beautiful. As soon as I held the crystals in my hands, I felt their vibrations throughout my body. Literally speaking, each stone was giving me so much love. I went on to doing my Crystalline Ascension Level Two workshop too. At the same time, I also have been taking healing sessions from Dr. Bala wherein I have been treated with A Grade therapeutic essential oils, as well as Light energy.

During the Crystalline Ascension Level One workshop, I experienced a wonderful cosmic attunement, wherein I felt the energy flowing through all my chakras. The Second Level workshop was even more enriching and fulfilling. I learned a beautiful technique called pendulum dowsing and also learned how to combine different crystals together in a grid formation in order to maximise their healing properties. I sincerely feel that after learning these various techniques, people can heal not only themselves, but also others and any situation in their lives. However, one must be ready for the change.

I work with my crystals everyday and it has been a most amazing experience. Despite pain or ailment, or no matter how tired I am, I have felt tremendous love from my crystals. Just holding them while in meditation or otherwise has completely energised me and made me feel totally vibrant and healthy. I feel fully connected with the Divine Light.

– Priya Shah

Case Study 5

I first heard of Dr. Gulrukh Bala's healing sessions in 2008 in Delhi.

A lot of inner turmoil including structural misalignment of my legs had been a constant growing concern, and I decided to visit Mumbai for a healing in June 2009.

At age four, I had fallen off a roof and sustained severe leg injuries. Several surgeries later, I learned to live my life with one leg an inch shorter than the other.

Dr. Bala received me with such compassion. She directed me to remain calm and assured me of Divine intervention. She worked on me through the hour even using A Grade Therapeutic Essential Oils and, when I arose, asked me to walk across the room. I did. My legs had received a complete healing! Structural balance and harmony after forty-five long years!

This is my most precious gift – a one of its kind experience which has deeply impacted me as well as my entire family.

My dear family friend's husband also went to Mumbai for crystalline healing sessions to release cancer cells and three healings later, the reports were all good.

My nephew has been for these deep core healings and his mental and emotional nature has transformed for life!

God bless!

– **Sonia Raj**

Case Study 6

2007.

I was most intrigued to hear stories of complete transformation through crystalline healing.

My growing anger and inner irritation forced me to take a good look and make a decision.

I went to Dr. Bala for a crystalline healing session.

She explained to me how it is all about my personal unshakeable intent and to focus on willing my healing. I was ready. I knew I was.

Life had been rough and I had handled it poorly. The session invigorated my being and awakened me to the knowledge of wasted years!

I had to take responsibility and work on inner change. I did. I attended more sessions and took her healing workshops.

Today, I stand confident and clear as life hands me her challenges. I value inner peace above all.

Deep gratitude, Dr. Bala.

— **Gautam Sanghi**

Case Study 7

July 2010.

I am a young lady of twenty-four, expecting my first baby. The sonography shows there is a blur around the two-month foetus, which denotes it has abnormalities and must be aborted.

I am completely shattered. The one glimmer of hope is to have a healing session with Dr. Bala. I have known her for three years and been a regular at her Saturday class with my family. I visit her and tell her my deepest feelings. I am sure of only one thing. I want this baby well and healthy. I am convulsed and in tears, I am so broken. She has felt what I am feeling and she says, "God is listening, come lie down and we will do a healing."

During the session, she told me she had witnessed the Divine Goddess's healing fingers conducting surgery inside my womb. I felt so hopeful and grateful.

I had another session three days later. And then Dr. Bala left for the US.

A week later, I had my next sonography taken and I took a second one too, to be certain. Both reports showed clarity. The blur had been cleared! My gynaecologist confirmed I could now have this baby. Something that modern medicine can hardly accomplish, Divine crystalline healing with prayer energies made it possible. I wrote to her immediately. I am in constant awe of the sessions experienced.

Deepest gratitude.

– **Deepti Singh**

QUICK REFERENCE

Appendix: Chrysolite.

Back: Lapis Lazuli, Malachite, Sapphire.

Bladder: Amber, Jasper, Topaz.

Bone Marrow: Fluorite.

Brain: Amber, Dark Blue Tourmaline, Green Tourmaline.

Circulatory System: Amethyst, Bloodstone, Hematite.

Digestive System: Green Jasper, Red Jade.

Ears: Amber, Calcite, Celestite, Orange.

Endocrine System: Amber, Amethyst, Fire Agate.

Eyes: Aquamarine, Blue Fluorite, Cat's Eye, Orange Calcite, Sapphire.

Fallopian Tubes: Chrysoprase.

Feet: Onyx, Smoky Quartz.

Female Reproductive System: Amber, Carnelian, Moonstone, Topaz.

Gall Bladder: Citrine, Jasper, Tiger's Eye, Topaz, Yellow Quartz.

Hands: Jadeite, Malachite.

Heart: Garnet, Rhodonite, Rose Quartz.

Immune System: Amethyst, Lapis Lazuli, Malachite, Turquoise.

Intestines: Beryl, Green Fluorite, Peridot.

Jaw: Aquamarine.

Joints: Azurite, Calcite.

Kidneys: Amber, Aquamarine, Bloodstone, Smoky Quartz.

Knees: Azurite, Jadeite.

Lower Back: Carnelian.

Lungs: Amber, Beryl, Emerald, Peridot, Turquoise.

Metabolism: Amethyst, Sodalite.

Muscle Tissue: Danburite, Magnetite.

Neck: Aquamarine, Quartz.

Nervous System: Amber, Green Jade, Green Tourmaline, Lapis Lazuli.

Pancreas: Blue Lace Agate, Red Tourmaline.

Pineal Gland: Gem Rhodonite.

Pituitary Gland: Pietersite.

Prostate Gland: Chrysoprase.

Shoulders: Selenite.

Skeletal System: Calcite, Fluorite, Iron Pyrite.

Spine: Beryl, Garnet, Tourmaline.

Spleen: Amber, Aquamarine, Bloodstone.

Stomach: Beryl, Green Fluorite.

Teeth: Aquamarine, Fluorite.

Testes: Carnelian, Topaz.

Throat: Amber, Aquamarine, Blue Tourmaline, Green Jasper, Lapis Lazuli.

Thymus: Aventurine, Blue Tourmaline.

Thyroid: Amber, Aquamarine, Citrine.

Veins: Snowflake Obsidian, Variscite.

ACKNOWLEDGEMENTS

I express eternal gratitude to the Source for the energy we continuously receive.

I wish to thank my beloved parents Naju and Jal Kapadia for their constant love and support, and my great ancestors and lineage whose blessings are showered upon us even today.

My darling Naushir and Farah, I am honoured that I have been graced with you as my children. I love you very much.

My precious siblings, Freny and Mahiyar, thank you for laughing with me, crying with me, and evolving with me.

I thank my dearest Rubinaz and Shahveer Cyrus Desai for their spontaneous support in providing photographs for crystal healing.

I thank my excellent photographers Rafeeq Ellias for the back cover photo, and Aresh Patel for all the crystal photographs in this book.

I thank Sylvia Theriault and Vidushi Arora for their invaluable presence through this project.

ACKNOWLEDGEMENTS

I thank my publisher Gautam Sachdeva for his belief
in me and in this book.

I also thank Shiv Sharma for editing and proof-reading
the text, and Girish Jathar and Sanjay Malandkar for their
pre-press work.

And all my friends, students and world family who are
awakeners – each and every one of you is special.

I am so grateful for the unfolding of each heart and each
soul Light journeying alongside me through time into
healing.

My deepest gratitude to our beloved Mother Earth, the
wind and water, fire and ether, for such patient allowing.

ABOUT THE AUTHOR

Initiated into Spiritual healing at an early age, Dr. Gulrukh Bala, Ph.D is the founder of Heartlight Ascension which is Supramental Yoga. Supramental means that one perceives an experience with every fibre of one's being; physical, mental, emotional and spiritual. It is 'knowing' in the most profound sense of the word, it is 'whole-istic' in that it is what is in its entirety, not just in part. There is complete freedom to create and manifest in the ability to see/feel/know oneself as part of the whole of all others.

Dr. Bala has been with in-depth holistic healing for twenty-five years. She is an enlightened counsellor, lifestyle motivator and workshop leader with dynamic interpersonal skills, addressing vital questions about how we can heal with a gathering of energies which are active around us at all times. She has to her credit a distinguished academic record in English Literature, Psychology and Holistic Healing multi-modalities.

After twelve years of teaching from home, Dr. Bala has chosen to fully devote her time to Heartlight Ascension which is the basic practice of connecting our flow of thought to the flow of breath. This training which goes beyond the mind is vital for maintaining clear energy centres.

Dr. Gulrukh Bala nurtures a unique blend of deep understanding of the Source in present day situations, helping thousands of people across the world to look inside beyond the mundane and reach higher levels of fulfilment.

Her workshops, weekly meditations, channelled healings and lecture tours are popular with CEOs, Border Security Force officials, therapists, teachers, professors, doctors, engineers, students, homemakers and young people, as Dr. Bala ushers in a new reality of peace, well-being, success and happiness for each one.

Dr. Gulrukh Bala offers multi-faceted seminars on Heartlight Ascension, Prosperity Consciousness, Dressing Our Present, Chakra Balancing, Meeting Our Spirit Guides, Crystalline Ascension, Essential Oils, Powerful Thought Affirmations and Visualisations, Channelled Readings, and One-on-One Healing and Counselling.

If you feel this book has been a guiding light and helped nurture your spirit, you may like to pay it forward by connecting to the A'hu Foundation work which helps improve lives even while augmenting our own.

You may also visit:
www.heartlightascension.com
www.twitter.com/gulrukhbala
www.speakingtree.com/drgulrukhbala
www.facebook.com/gulrukhbala
Blog: www.drgulrukhbala.com

BIBLIOGRAPHY

Diane Stein: *The Women's Spirituality Book,* Llewellyn Publications, 1980.

Edgar Cayce: *The Power of Colour, Stones and Crystals,* Warner Books, 1989.

Katrina Raphaell: *The Crystalline Transmission – A Synthesis of Light,* Vol. 3, Aurora Press, 1989.

Phyllis Galde: *Crystal Healing, The Next Step,* Llewellyn Publications, 1980.

Scott Cunningham: *Encyclopedia of Crystal, Gem and Metal Magic* – Llewellyn Publications, 1997.

Stephanie and Tim Harrison: *Crystal Therapy* – Element Books Ltd., 2000.

Judy Hall: *The Crystal Bible* – Godsfield Press, 2003.

The author may be contacted by email:
drgulrukhbala@gmail.com
www.heartlightascension.com
Tel: (022) 23827812 (8 to 9 am and 9 to 10 pm only)

Audio downloads of Dr. Gulrukh Bala's
'Healing Meditations' are available on
www.yogiimpressions.com

For further details, contact:
Yogi Impressions Books Pvt. Ltd.
1711, Centre 1, World Trade Centre,
Cuffe Parade, Mumbai 400 005, India.

Fill in the Mailing List form on our website
and receive, via email, information on
books, authors, events and more.
Visit: www.yogiimpressions.com

Telephone: (022) 22155036/7/8
Fax: (022) 22155039
E-mail: yogi@yogiimpressions.com

 Join us on Facebook:
www.facebook.com/yogiimpressions

 Follow us on Twitter:
www.twitter.com/yogiimpressions

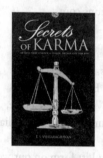

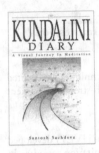

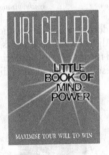

AUDIO CDs

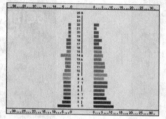
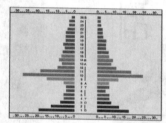

NOTES